my **revision** notes

OCR GCSE

COMPUTER SCIENCE

George Rouse

HODDER
EDUCATION
AN HACHETTE UK COMPANY

The Publishers would like to thank the following for permission to reproduce copyright material.

Acknowledgements and Photo credits

p.11 © Sergey Jarochkin/123RF; **p.16** © mingis/istock/thinkstock; **p.24** © Editorial Image, LLC/Alamy; **p.25** © inga spence/Alamy; **p.45** *top* © Rob Bartee/Alamy; *bottom* © B Christopher/ Alamy Stock Photo; **p. 55** © Bloomberg/gettyimages; **p. 56** © Peter Essick/Aurora Photos/Corbis; **p.100** *both* © George Rouse.

Blu-ray Disc™ is a trademark owned by Blu-ray Disc Association (BDA).

UNIX is a registered trademark of The Open Group.

Mac and OS X are trademarks of Apple Inc., registered in the U.S. and other countries.

Python is a trademark or registered trademark of the Python Software Foundation, used by Hodder & Stoughton with permission from the Foundation.

Although every effort has been made to ensure that website addresses are correct at time of going to press, Hodder Education cannot be held responsible for the content of any website mentioned in this book. It is sometimes possible to find a relocated web page by typing in the address of the home page for a website in the URL window of your browser.

Hachette UK's policy is to use papers that are natural, renewable and recyclable products and made from wood grown in sustainable forests. The logging and manufacturing processes are expected to conform to the environmental regulations of the country of origin.

Orders:
please contact Bookpoint Ltd, 130 Milton Park, Abingdon, Oxon OX14 4SE.
tel: +44 (0)1235 827720
fax: +44 (0)1235 400454
e-mail: education@bookpoint.co.uk Lines are open from 9 a.m. to 5 p.m., Monday to Saturday, with a 24-hour message answering service. You can also order through our website: www.hoddereducation.co.uk

ISBN: 978 1 4718 8665 2

© George Rouse 2017

First published in 2017 by
Hodder Education,
An Hachette UK Company

Carmelite House

50 Victoria Embankment

London EC4Y 0DZ

www.hoddereducation.co.uk

Impression number   10   9   8   7   6   5   4   3   2   1
Year   2021   2020   2019   2018   2017

Cover photo © cosmin4000/Thinkstock/Getty Images

Illustrations by

Typeset in Bembo Std Regular 11/13 pt by Aptara, Inc.

Printed in

A catalogue record for this title is available from the British Library.

Get the most from this book

Everyone has to decide his or her own revision strategy, but it is essential to review your work, learn it and test your understanding. These Revision Notes will help you to do that in a planned way, topic by topic. Use this book as the cornerstone of your revision and don't hesitate to write in it – personalise your notes and check your progress by ticking off each section as you revise.

Tick to track your progress

Use the revision planner on page 4 to plan your revision, topic by topic. Tick each box when you have:

- revised and understood a topic
- tested yourself
- checked your answers.

You can also keep track of your revision by ticking off each topic heading in the book. You may find it helpful to add your own notes as you work through each topic.

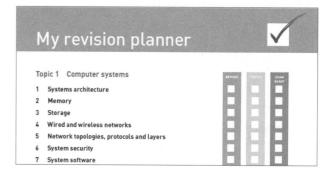

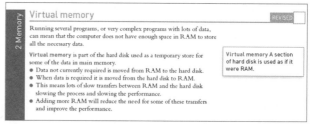

Features to help you succeed

Worked examples

Several worked examples are given for some topics.

Key terms

Key terms are highlighted in each section.

Exam tips

Expert tips are given throughout the book to help you polish your exam technique in order to maximise your chances in the exam.

Exam-style questions

Practice exam questions are provided for each topic. Use them to consolidate your revision and practise your exam skills.

Answers

Check how you've done using the answers at the back of the book.

My revision planner

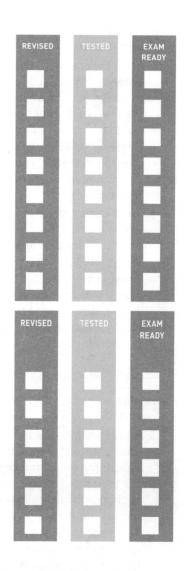

Countdown to my exams

6–8 weeks to go

- Start by looking at the specification — make sure you know exactly what material you need to revise and the style of the examination. Use the revision planner on page 5 of this book to familiarise yourself with the topics.
- Organise your notes, making sure you have covered everything on the specification. The revision planner will help you to group your notes into topics.
- Work out a realistic revision plan that will allow you time for relaxation. Set aside days and times for all the subjects that you need to study, and stick to your timetable.
- Set yourself sensible targets. Break your revision down into focused sessions of around 40 minutes, divided by breaks. These Revision Notes organise the basic facts into short, memorable sections to make revising easier.

REVISED ☐

2–6 weeks to go

- Read through the relevant sections of this book and refer to the exam tips, exam summaries, typical mistakes and key terms. Tick off the topics as you feel confident about them. Highlight those topics you find difficult and look at them again in detail.
- Test your understanding of each topic by working through the 'Now test yourself' questions in the book. Look up the answers at the back of the book.
- Make a note of any problem areas as you revise, and ask your teacher to go over these in class.
- Look at past papers. They are one of the best ways to revise and practise your exam skills. Write or prepare planned answers to the exam practice questions provided in this book. Check your answers with those at the back of this book.
- Try out different revision methods. For example, you can make notes using mind maps, spider diagrams or flash cards.
- Track your progress using the revision planner and give yourself a reward when you have achieved your target.

REVISED ☐

One week to go

- Try to fit in at least one more timed practice of an entire past paper and seek feedback from your teacher, comparing your work closely with the mark scheme.
- Check the revision planner to make sure you haven't missed out any topics. Brush up on any areas of difficulty by talking them over with a friend or getting help from your teacher.
- Attend any revision classes put on by your teacher. Remember, he or she is an expert at preparing people for examinations.

REVISED ☐

The day before the examination

- Flick through these Revision Notes for useful reminders, for example the exam tips, exam summaries, typical mistakes and key terms.
- Check the time and place of your examination.
- Make sure you have everything you need — extra pens and pencils, tissues, a watch, bottled water, sweets.
- Allow some time to relax and have an early night to ensure you are fresh and alert for the examinations.

REVISED ☐

My exams

Computer Science Paper 1

Date:...

Time:...

Location:..

Computer Science Paper 2

Date:...

Time:...

Location:..

Topic 1

Computer systems

1 Systems architecture

Computer hardware

Hardware is the term that describes the physical components of a computer system.

The computer inputs, processes, stores and outputs data.

The computer hardware works with software to process data.

The CPU

The **CPU** is responsible for completing all the processing in the computer by following a set of instructions.

The CPU works at incredible speeds governed by the clock chip.
- The clock chip is a vibrating crystal that maintains a constant speed.
- Modern CPUs can work at speeds around 4 GHz (4 000 000 000) instructions per second.

Computer architecture The internal, logical structure and organisation of the computer hardware.

Central processing unit (CPU) Carries out all the processing in a computer.

Now test yourself

1 What is the purpose of the CPU in a computer?
2 What is meant by the clock speed of a computer?

Von Neumann architecture

John von Neumann designed a computer architecture in which:
- data and instructions are both stored in the same memory
- all instructions and data are stored in binary.

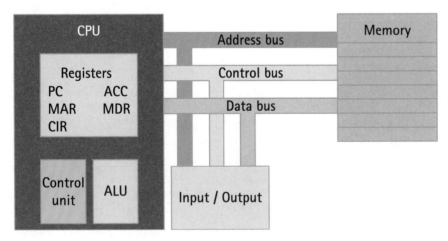

Figure 1.1 Simplified diagram of the CPU, buses and memory

This design creates a model of the CPU which will include these elements.

Arithmetic and logic unit (ALU)

The **arithmetic and logic unit** carries out the calculations and logical decisions required by the program instruction. (For example addition, subtraction and comparisons such as equal to, greater than or less than.)

Control unit (CU)

The **control unit** is responsible for decoding the instructions. It sends out signals to control how data moves around the parts of the CPU and memory to execute these instructions.

Registers

Registers are very fast access memory locations in the CPU. There are a number of registers that are temporary data stores in the CPU, which include the:

- **accumulator** stores the results of any calculations made by the arithmetic and logic unit (ALU).
- **program counter** keeps track of the memory location for the **next** instruction to be dealt with.
- **memory address register** stores the location in memory to be used, i.e. where to locate data it needs to fetch or where to send data it needs to store.
- **memory data register** is used to store any data fetched from memory or any data that is to be transferred to and stored in memory.

> **Arithmetic and logic unit (ALU)** Performs all the arithmetic and logical operations in the CPU.
>
> **Control unit** Controls the flow of data within the CPU and decodes instructions.

> **Accumulator (ACC)** Temporary store for the results from the ALU.
>
> **Program Counter (PC)** Stores the address of the next instruction to be processed.
>
> **Memory Address Register (MAR)** Stores the address for data to be fetched from or sent to memory.
>
> **Memory Data Register (MDR)** Stores data that has been fetched from or is to be sent to memory.

Now test yourself

TESTED ☐

3 What are the features of the Von Neumann computer architecture?
4 What is the function of
   (a) the MAR
   (b) the accumulator
   (c) the ALU
   in a CPU?

> **Exam tip**
>
> You should learn what each of these registers does and what data they store and when.

Fetch–decode–execute cycle

The CPU continually fetches, decodes and executes instructions.

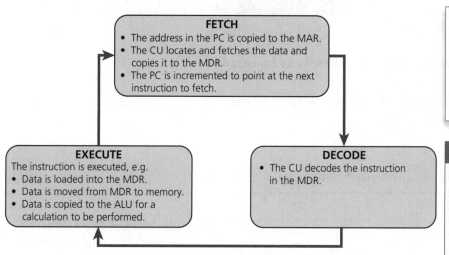

FETCH
- The address in the PC is copied to the MAR.
- The CU locates and fetches the data and copies it to the MDR.
- The PC is incremented to point at the next instruction to fetch.

DECODE
- The CU decodes the instruction in the MDR.

EXECUTE
The instruction is executed, e.g.
- Data is loaded into the MDR.
- Data is moved from MDR to memory.
- Data is copied to the ALU for a calculation to be performed.

Figure 1.2 Fetch–decode–execute cycle

> **Fetch–decode–execute cycle** The process of fetching instructions from memory decoding and executing them performed continuously by the CPU.

> **Exam tip**
>
> You need to know what happens at each stage of the fetch–decode–execute cycle. Note this is sometimes just called the fetch–execute cycle, but it means exactly the same.

Now test yourself

5 Describe what changes happen to the PC during the fetch–decode–execute cycle.
6 What is the function of the control unit in the fetch–decode–execute cycle?

Cache

As well as the registers, the CPU will have some very fast memory (cache) used to store frequently used data and instructions waiting to be dealt with.

● **Cache memory** is located very close to the CPU with dedicated connections to provide very fast access to the data.
● Cache memory is very expensive compared to the main memory units in a computer so is generally much smaller in size than main memory.

> **Cache memory** Fast memory used by the CPU to store data required by the CPU.

There are three 'levels' of cache available, L1, L2 and L3.

	Distance from processor	Access speed	Cost	Capacity
L1	usually located on the CPU itself	similar to the main registers on the CPU	most expensive	smallest capacity
L2	usually located on the CPU itself but further away than L1	almost as fast as L1		
L3	usually located away from the CPU on the computer motherboard	slowest, though still much faster than main memory	least expensive	largest capacity

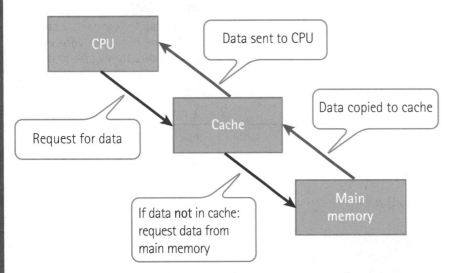

Figure 1.3 Cache memory is used to store data waiting to be processed

Common characteristics of CPUs that affect their performance

Cache memory

Having more and faster cache memory will provide the CPU with faster access to data.

Clock speed

The more instructions that can be completed per second, the faster the data can be processed.

> **Clock speed** The number of instruction the CPU can carry out per second.

Number of cores

If a processor has multiple cores, each core can fetch, decode and execute instructions at the same time and can handle more instructions simultaneously. For example, a **multi-core** processor can run more than one program at the same time.

A dual core processor has two cores and quad core, four, so the more cores the faster the CPU can process instructions.

A typical quad-core processor will have L1, L2 and L3 cache.

L1 and L2 cache will be provided for each core and L3 cache will be shared.

Core 0	Core 1	Core 2	Core 3
L1 Cache	L1 Cache	L1 Cache	L1 Cache
L2 Cache	L2 Cache	L2 Cache	L2 Cache
Inclusive shared L3 Cache			

Figure 1.4 A typical multi-core processor arrangement with L1, L2 and L3 cache

> **Multi-core** A CPU with multiple processors.

> **Exam tip**
>
> You need to be aware of the contribution each of these items has to the performance of the computer. Note twice as many cores can potentially double the number of instructions per second.

Now test yourself

TESTED

7 What is cache memory?
8 How does the number of cores in a CPU affect the performance?

Embedded systems

REVISED

An embedded computer is a computer system that has a dedicated function as part of a larger system.

These are often manufactured as a single chip (micro-computer) or by combining several separate integrated circuits for processing, memory and interfacing within a larger device.

> **Embedded system** A dedicated computer system that is part of an electronic device.

Figure 1.5 A microcontroller

Embedded systems are found in most consumer products, such as washing machines, microwaves or car engine management systems.
- Embedded systems can be designed and engineered to reduce the size and improve performance.
- Programs are often loaded at the manufacturing stage or uploaded directly.
- There are either no, or very limited, options to modify these programs through a simple interface.

Figure 1.6 **This washing machine uses an embedded system**

The dedicated hardware and software make embedded systems significantly more reliable and robust than would be the case with general-purpose computer systems.

Embedded systems can be:
- low power devices so they can operate effectively from a small power source, for example in a mobile phone
- small in size to fit inside a wrist worn device such as a fitness bracelet
- rugged so they can be used in a wide range of applications such as car engine management or avionics
- low cost, making them suitable for use in mass-produced items, such as the controller in a washing machine or set-top box
- dedicated to just one task with dedicated interfaces and software, for example in computer-aided manufacturing systems.

Exam practice

1 (a) Explain how cache size affects the speed of a computer.
  (b) Describe two other factors that affect the speed of a computer.
2 Describe what is stored in the MDR (Memory Data Register) during the fetch–decode–execute cycle.
3 Identify and describe the features of an embedded system that make it suitable for use in a small 'drone' helicopter device.

ONLINE

Summary

You should now have an understanding of the following:
- Computer hardware is the physical components of a computer system.
- The CPU carries out all the processing for the computer.
- Von Neumann architecture is a model where data and instructions are stored in binary in the same memory. This is the model for most computer systems.

- The CPU includes a number of fast access memory locations including registers and cache memory.
- The factors that affect the performance of the CPU are clock speed, cache, number of cores.
- Embedded systems are dedicated computer systems that form part of an electronic device.

2 Memory

- When the computer is on, the operating system and any utilities and data required to run the computer are stored in primary memory.
- When a program is loaded to a computer it, and any data it uses, are also stored in primary memory.

RAM and ROM

Random access memory (RAM)

Random access memory (RAM)is **volatile memory**, which needs power to maintain it; if the power is turned off then RAM loses its content.
- RAM is the main memory in a computer.
- RAM holds the operating system, applications and data currently in use by the computer.
- The CPU can access RAM very quickly and access times are much faster than those for secondary storage, e.g. hard disk.
- The more RAM in a computer, the more programs and data it can keep available, i.e. more RAM implies improved performance.

Data is transferred from secondary storage to RAM to cache to the CPU

> **Volatile memory** Loses all data when there is no power.

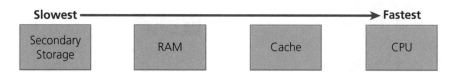

Slowest ———————————————→ Fastest

| Secondary Storage | RAM | Cache | CPU |

Figure 2.1 Data transfer speeds

Read-only memory (ROM)

Read-only memory (ROM) is **non-volatile memory**, which does NOT need power to maintain it; if the power is turned off then ROM keeps its content.
- ROM provides storage for data and instructions for starting up and initialising the computer. (The boot process.)
- ROM is called read-only memory because the computer cannot overwrite its content.
- Information stored in ROM is usually programmed by the manufacturer.

> **Non-volatile memory** Able to retain data without the need for external power.

Now test yourself

1 What is the difference between RAM and ROM?
2 What is stored in RAM while a computer is working?
3 What is stored in ROM?

Virtual memory

Running several programs, or very complex programs with lots of data, can mean that the computer does not have enough space in RAM to store all the necessary data.

Virtual memory is part of the hard disk used as a temporary store for some of the data in main memory.

- Data not currently required is moved from RAM to the hard disk.
- When data is required it is moved from the hard disk to RAM.
- This means lots of slow transfers between RAM and the hard disk slowing the process and slowing the performance.
- Adding more RAM will reduce the need for some of these transfers and improve the performance.

> **Virtual memory** A section of hard disk is used as if it were RAM.

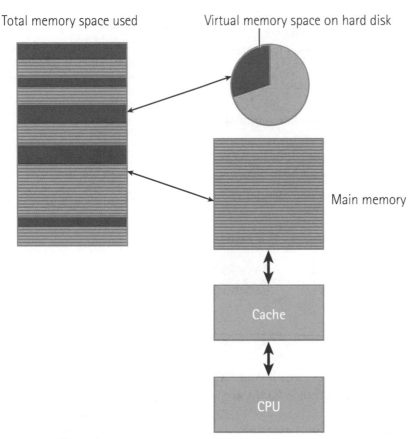

Figure 2.2 **Virtual memory**

> **Exam tip**
>
> This is a major factor affecting the performance of a computer system beyond the factors affecting the speed of the CPU. While the computer specification determines these other factors, more RAM can usually be added to improve performance.

Flash memory

Flash memory is a special type of ROM that can be written to by the computer.

- Flash memory is solid-state memory and is used in portable or removable devices to store data.
- It is faster than a magnetic hard disk but slower than RAM.

> **Exam tip**
>
> Solid-state devices using flash memory are also commonly used as the secondary storage in a range of hand-held devices and larger computer systems.

Exam practice

Shirley's computer has 2 GB of RAM and a 200 GB hard disk. Shirley uses her computer for working on her accounts using a spreadsheet; advertising using a desktop publishing package; listening to music and keeping track of email. It is running quite slowly. Suggest what might be causing it to run slowly and explain how the performance might be improved.

ONLINE

Summary

You should now have an understanding of the following:

A computer uses two types of main memory:

- RAM is volatile and data is lost when the power is turned off
- RAM holds the operating system, any applications and data while the computer is working
- ROM is non-volatile memory, which retains data when the power is turned off
- ROM holds the settings and sequences required to start the computer when the power is turned on
- ROM contents cannot be overwritten by the computer and are often programmed by the manufacturer.

Virtual memory uses part of the hard disk to supplement the RAM:

- data not currently required by the process is moved to a section of the hard disk and data that is required is moved from hard disk to RAM
- virtual memory requires a lot of slow transfers between RAM and the hard disk slowing the performance of the computer
- adding more RAM can reduce the use of virtual memory and improve the performance of the computer.

Flash or solid-state memory is a special type of ROM that can be written to by the computer.

- Flash memory is commonly used in portable devices.
- Flash memory transfer speeds are better than the hard disk but lower than RAM.

3 Storage

Most computer systems require access to several programs that can be used as required.

It is not possible to store these in RAM since it is volatile and all the data is lost when the power is turned off.

While it can store programs when the power is turned off, ROM cannot be written to and cannot have new programs or data written to it by the computer. While this is reasonable for an embedded system that only ever runs a small number of fixed programs, for most computer systems we need access to a range of programs.

Without secondary storage, computers could only use a fixed number of programs or programs typed in every time they were required, and could not store any data.

Typically the secondary **storage device** on a general-purpose computer will store the operating system, applications (programs) and the user's data.

> **Storage device** The hardware used to read from and write to **storage media**.
>
> **Storage media** The media data is saved on and retrieved from.

Types of secondary storage REVISED

Magnetic hard drives

Magnetic hard disks are the most common type of secondary storage in general-purpose computer systems.
- They use a stack of magnetic platters that rotate.
- A moving read/write head hovers above the surface and can move in and out over the platters to read the data.
- Magnetic disks are a reliable and cost-effective form of secondary storage providing high capacity at low cost.

Figure 3.1 A hard disk drive showing the platters and heads

Solid-state drives

Solid-state drives (SSD) use flash memory and are commonly used in hand-held devices and increasingly within general-purpose computer systems.

- SSDs use flash memory and have no moving parts making them robust and ideally suited for use in portable devices.
- With no moving parts, there are no delays in accessing parts of the drive, making access to data faster than for a magnetic hard disk.
- Having no moving parts means SSDs have lower power requirements and do not generate any heat or noise when in use.
- SSDs are lightweight, making them ideal for use in hand-held devices.
- SSDs have typically smaller capacity than magnetic hard disks and the cost per unit of storage is higher.

SSDs are used in:

- USB storage devices commonly used for storing and transferring files between computers
- tablet computers and other hand-held computing devices to store data and programs
- cameras to store images
- general-purpose computers as the main secondary storage.

Exam tip

For archive storage of large amounts of data, magnetic tapes are still in use because they can store huge amounts of data at very low cost, but access is very slow and specialised equipment is required to read from and write to this medium.

Hybrid drives

The hybrid drive uses both magnetic hard disks and solid-state memory.

- This type of drive uses the low-cost storage capacities of magnetic hard disks with the access speeds of solid-state to provide cost-effective but fast secondary storage.
- Frequently used data stored on the magnetic disk is transferred to the solid-state device improving the access times for this data and the overall performance of the drive.

Optical drives

- Optical disk devices use laser light reflecting from the surface of a rotating reflective disk to read data.

CD-ROM/DVD-ROM are read-only media.

- These are commercially pressed disks with small dips in the surface, called pits, which are detected by a sensor when the laser light is reflected from the surface.

CD-R and DVD-R are write-once/read-many-times media.

- These are blank media that can be written to (burned) by a CD writer device but cannot be written to again, making them ideal for distributing data.

CD-RW and DVD-RW are rewriteable media.

- These are blank media that can be written to many times making them ideal for backing up and transferring data.
- Writeable media have a layer of dye that can be changed by shining a laser light onto it. The change in colour mimics the pits in the surface on commercially pressed CDs/DVDs so that they can be read by a standard CD/DVD drive.

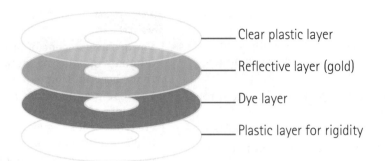

Clear plastic layer

Reflective layer (gold)

Dye layer

Plastic layer for rigidity

Figure 3.2 An exploded view of a CD-RW showing the layers

The Blu-ray Disc™ is an optical device that uses blue light, which can detect data stored at a much higher density than the red light used for CD and DVD media.

● Blu-ray media can be formatted with up to four layers.
● They are available as read only or read/write media

Optical media are an ideal way of distributing data; they are low cost and robust.

Optical media are ideal for archive storage for large amounts of data at low cost.

Table 3.1 Comparison of optical media

Media	Typical capacity
CD	700 MB
DVD	4.7 GB
Blu-ray	25 GB per layer

> **Exam tip**
>
> Note: a device is the hardware that reads and writes the data to the medium.
>
> For example, a DVD drive is a device that reads from or writes to the media, CD/DVD. Try to use the right words when describing these.

Choosing the right media

REVISED

When selecting the right device or media for a purpose, the following must be taken into account.

● Capacity: how much data does it need to store?
● Speed: how quickly does the data need to be accessed?
● Portability: does the device or media need to be transported?
  ○ If so the size and weight are important.
● Durability: will the device or media be used in a hostile environment?
  ○ If so the media must be resistant to external shocks or extreme conditions.
● Reliability: does it need to be used repeatedly without failing?
● Cost: what is the cost per unit of storage related to the value of the data?

> **Exam tip**
>
> With the improvement in broadband speeds and the availability of online file storage, it is often cheaper and significantly faster to transfer files using the cloud. Consider whether it is acceptable in the context of the question to suggest this method for transferring files rather than a CD or DVD when many computers no longer have built-in drives for these media.

In order to calculate the capacity requirements, knowing what is being stored on the media is important. The table below shows the typical size for some common files.

File type	Approximate size
1-page word-processed file with no images	100 KB
postcard-size photograph	6 MB
3-minute MP3 music track	6 MB
3-minute music track on a music CD	50 MB
1-minute MPEG video	50 MB
DVD film	4 GB
high-definition film	8–15 GB
Blu-ray film	20–25 GB
4k high-resolution film	100 GB or more

Example

To store 50 × 3-minute MP3 music tracks the size of the data is:

50 × 6 MB = 300 MB   which will fit easily onto a standard CD-RW.

To store a 90-minute MPEG video

90 × 50 MB = 4500 MB or 4.5 GB requiring a DVD-RW

Now test yourself

1 What is stored on the hard disk in a personal computer?
2 What are the advantages of SSDs over magnetic hard disks?
3 What is the most suitable media for distributing high-definition video films?
4 Identify three factors to consider when choosing secondary storage media and devices.
5 How much space do I need to store 200 postcard-size photographic images and what is the most suitable medium if these are to be sent to another person?

The rate at which data can be transferred will also be a factor in the decision:

Storage type	Transfer rate (typical)
RAM	12–20 GB/s
SSD	200–550 MB/s
Magnetic hard disk	50–120 MB/s
Blu-ray Disc	72 MB/s
USB flash drive	45–90 MB/s
DVD	1.32 MB/s
CD	0.146 MB/s

Exam practice

1 What is the purpose of secondary storage in a computer system?
2 Identify what would be the most suitable secondary storage medium for a computer used by an engineer on a North Sea oil rig and explain why.
3 Sandra wants to copy files from her computer to send to a friend. Calculate the total size of the files and identify the most suitable media.
   2 × 5-minute MPEG videos
   3 × 3-minute MP3 music files
   3 × postcard-size photographs

ONLINE

Summary

You should now have an understanding of the following:

- Secondary storage is needed to store data and programs that would otherwise be lost when the power was turned off.
- Magnetic hard disks are high-capacity, low-cost but relatively slow-access devices commonly used on general-purpose computers including personal and commercial systems.
- Solid-state devices are available in a range of capacities from small portable USB memory devices to internal memory in hand-held devices to reasonably large solid-state disk drives in general-purpose computers. Access is faster than a hard disk drive but they are more expensive and lower capacity than magnetic hard disk drives. Flash memory is small, fast and robust.
- Optical disks are storage media that use light to read and write data. They are low cost, robust, light and portable making them ideal for distributing data and applications.

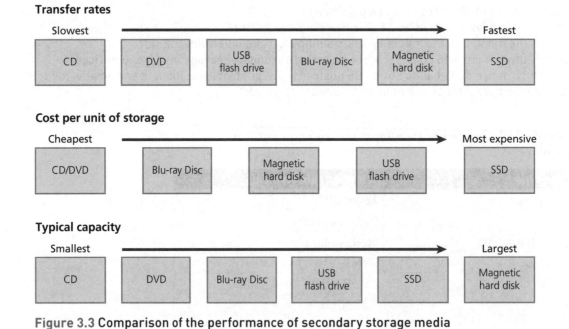

Transfer rates

Slowest					Fastest
CD	DVD	USB flash drive	Blu-ray Disc	Magnetic hard disk	SSD

Cost per unit of storage

Cheapest				Most expensive
CD/DVD	Blu-ray Disc	Magnetic hard disk	USB flash drive	SSD

Typical capacity

Smallest					Largest
CD	DVD	Blu-ray Disc	USB flash drive	SSD	Magnetic hard disk

Figure 3.3 Comparison of the performance of secondary storage media

4 Wired and wireless networks

A network is a collection of computer systems linked together.

The advantages of this are:
- work can be shared out between nodes
- easy communication between users
- files can be shared
- peripheral devices can be shared
- centralised administration and updates
- user activity can be monitored.
- users can login to any connected computer.

Types of network

Wide area network

A wide area network (WAN) covers a large geographical area and can take in many cities or countries.

A telecoms company will provide the connections between the computer systems or groups of computer systems.

Local area network

A local area network (LAN) covers a small geographical area, for example a single building or group of buildings.

The owner of the LAN usually owns the entire infrastructure and provides all the network support and administration.

Client–server networks

Client–server networks are the most common way to organise a LAN.

A number of computers are designated as servers to provide services for the rest of the network.

Servers are usually high-specification computers that look after:
● user logins
● security
● file handling
● internet access.

There may be a number of servers on a LAN providing different services, for example a file server and an email server.

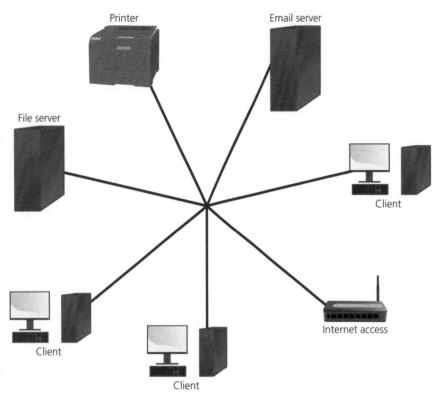

Figure 4.1 A client–server network

Advantages	Disadvantages
Files are stored centrally so easily located and tracked.	Expensive to set up.
System can be backed up centrally.	Difficult to maintain requiring specialist support.
Software can be installed and updated centrally.	Dependent upon server: if the server fails, the system will not work.
Good security features, e.g. personal login and password, different access levels for user groups, centralised anti-malware software.	
Centralised file server means fewer duplicated files and applications.	

Peer-to-peer networks

Peer-to-peer networks do not have servers

- all computers have equal status
- each computer can share files with the others at the owner's discretion
- they are easy to set up and do not rely on a server for any services
- security can be an issue
- peer-to-peer networks are suitable for small home installations
- larger peer-to-peer systems are used to share files, often illegally, using the internet.

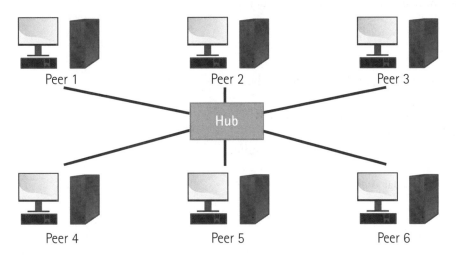

Figure 4.2 **A peer-to-peer network**

Advantages	Disadvantages
Easy to set up, simply connect to other devices on the network directly. Limited costs involved with no file server required. Does not depend upon the server so continues to work when another device fails.	No centralised administration or management, security and updates must be dealt with separately for each node. Poor traffic management can slow individual machines when they are being accessed, or the network as a whole, when there is excessive traffic. Peer computers may be less reliable than a properly maintained server. Dispersed nature means many files and applications are duplicated.

Now test yourself

TESTED

1 What is the difference between a LAN and a WAN?
2 Identify two advantages of a client–server organisation for a LAN.
3 Identify two advantages of a peer-to-peer network.

Network hardware

REVISED

Network interface cards

Network interface cards (NIC) are required to connect a device to the network, although these are almost always part of the device's motherboard.

- A NIC provides the electrical signals to send data and also deals with data that is received.
- The NIC uses a protocol for the network it is attached to in order to send and receive data.

Network switches

These connect the devices together by sending packets of data to the required destination.

- Switches are usually self-learning and create a table of connected devices to route the data to its destination.
- Switches use the MAC address (media access control address, a unique identifier allocated to the device at the manufacturing stage that cannot be changed) of the device to identify what is connected to it.

Routers

Routers are used to send packets of data between networks.

- Routers are used to connect networks to the internet.
- Routers create tables of routes to destinations and make the decision about which path between nodes to use.

Transmission media

REVISED

Wireless networks

Wireless networks, often using **WiFi**, use radio signals to connect devices.

- Wireless access points connect wireless devices to a network.
- These normally connect to a router, but it is common to include a router and wireless access point in the same unit.

> **WiFi** A common standard for wireless connectivity.

Wired networks

Wired networks use copper or fibre **Ethernet** cables to connect devices by making a physical connection.

- They often use Cat 5 or Cat 6 cables.
- Cat 5 and Cat 6 cables are known as **UTP cables (unshielded twisted pair).**

Another form of copper cable is the coaxial cable.

- Coaxial cable is bulkier than UTP and more difficult to install.

> **Ethernet** A set of standards used to connect devices in a LAN.
>
> **UTP (unshielded twisted pair)** A common connecting cable using copper wires with each pair of wires twisted around each other to minimise interference between the cables.

Figure 4.3 UTP Cable

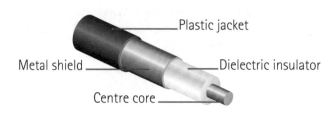

Plastic jacket

Metal shield

Dielectric insulator

Centre core

Figure 4.4 Coaxial cable

Fibre-optic networks

Fibre-optic cable transmits signals as light along glass fibres.

- The signal in fibre-optic cable does not deteriorate quickly making it ideal for cabling over long distances.
- Fibre-optic cable is not subject to interference from neighbouring cables.
- Fibre-optic cable is suited to use in exposed locations.

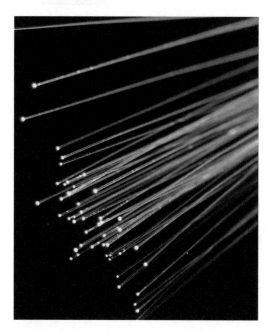

Figure 4.5 Fibre-optic cable

Wired or wireless?

Wired	Wireless
Transmission speeds are much faster than wireless ones.	Since wireless transmission rates are quite slow it can be problematic when several users are sharing a connection.
Wired networks can be difficult and expensive to install.	Wireless networks are easy and cheap to install with no need for trunking, wall-mounted boxes, holes in walls etc.
Wired network are reasonably secure.	It is possible to intercept a wireless signal so extra security is required when setting up a wireless network.

Now test yourself

TESTED

4 Why is fibre-optic cable chosen by telecoms companies to deliver internet connections to customers?
5 Identify one advantage of a wired network over a wireless one.

The internet

The internet is worldwide collection of networks, a network of networks.

The use of agreed standards has made it possible for a diverse range of systems to communicate with each other.

The World Wide Web

The World Wide Web is a collection of websites hosted on various servers connected to the internet.

The locations of these websites are IP addresses such as 69.172.201.167

> **Exam tip**
>
> Note: the internet is not the same as the World Wide Web.

Domain Name Server

A domain name server (DNS) can translate these IP addresses into an easier-to-remember URL (uniform resource locator) such as www.hodder.co.uk

- When you type in a URL, it is forwarded to the DNS to look up the IP address.
- If the DNS does not know the IP address for the URL, it will forward it to another DNS and so on until it finds (or does not find) the IP address.

Domain name system

A domain name system is hierarchical and starts with a top-level domain such as:

- com: commercial business
- uk: UK based
- fr: based in France.

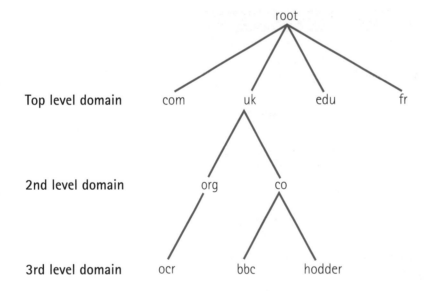

Figure 4.6 **A hierarchical naming system**

Host

A host is a computer that stores a particular resource.

The computer that stores the Hodder newsletters is located by looking up the IP address for www.hodder.co.uk on a DNS.

Once that is located it is able to retrieve the specific item we require.

Figure 4.7 Structure of a URL

Figure 4.8 Website accessed by URL in Figure 4.7

The cloud

The cloud is the term we use to describe remote provision of storage and software resources.

The cloud uses servers and data centres located worldwide and connected to the internet.

Cloud services have many benefits:
- no need to update software accessed from these remote providers
- access to data and applications from any internet-connected computer
- no need to worry about data being backed up
- easy to share files with colleagues worldwide
- no need to maintain your own network to store data
- no need for expensive support staff.

There are a number of issues:
- you are entrusting your data to someone outside your organisation
- you trust that your data will be stored safely and securely
- you trust that the service will be there when you need it
- some of these servers and data centres are in countries with different legislation meaning sensitive data might not be secure.

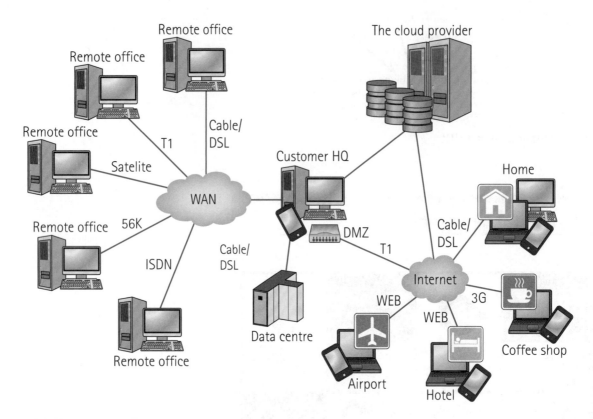

Figure 4.9 Cloud computing

Virtual networks

Virtual networks are connected devices that do not make up a discrete physical domain. Data is accessible to a selection of computers on the LAN or WAN.

A common way to implement a virtual network is to use services provided on the internet.
- A virtual network allows the users to access and use software and data located on servers or computers over the internet.
- Virtual networks are often accessed via a web browser.
- Remote services and devices can be accessed as if they were part of the hardware in a LAN.

Virtual networks may be subsets of existing LANs known as VLANs.

The computers may be on a single LAN or on several connected LANs.

Example

In a large organisation with branches in several countries the accounts department computers in each location may be connected into a single virtual network so that files can be shared by accounts staff but are not available to others on the physical network.

Now test yourself

6 What does a DNS do?
7 Identify one advantage and one disadvantage to an organisation for using the cloud to provide software services.

Exam practice

A small accountancy firm uses several stand-alone computers. The manager is thinking of networking these machines and connecting them to the internet.
1 Describe three hardware items required to do this.
2 Describe two advantages to the accountancy firm of networking their computers.
3 Describe one advantage and one disadvantage of using a wireless network.

ONLINE

Summary

You should now have an understanding of the following:

A network is a collection of connected computer devices.
- A LAN is a local area network based in a small geographical area.
- A WAN is a wide area network covering a large geographical area.

Client–server is a common way to organise a LAN using servers to provide services for the connected devices.

Peer-to-peer networks use direct connections between computer devices.

The hardware required to set up a network includes:
- a NIC (network interface card) to manage the electrical signals to and from the network
- a switch to route traffic on the network
- a router to connect different networks together

- a wireless access point to connect devices using radio signals
- cables for wired networks to connect devices.

The internet is a collection of connected computer devices.

The World Wide Web is a collection of websites accessed using the internet.

A DNS (domain name server) converts easily identifiable URL names into a physical IP address.

A host is a computer that stores resources on the internet.

The cloud is a term we use to describe remote provision of storage and software resources.

A virtual network is a collection of computer devices on a LAN or WAN acting as a discrete network.

5 Network topologies, protocols and layers

Topologies REVISED

Star networks

The star is the most common network arrangement.
● All nodes are connected to a central switch or hub.
● Star networks tend to be fast and reliable since each device has its own connection to the central device.
● Another advantage of this layout is that it minimises data collisions.

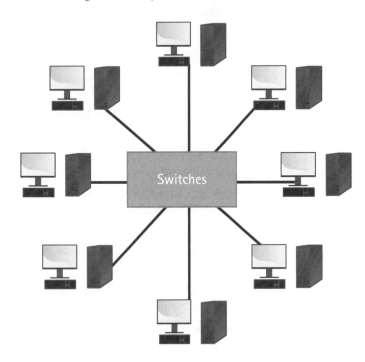

Figure 5.1 A star network layout

Mesh networks

A mesh topology uses direct connections between the nodes.
● Each node has multiple connections, via other nodes to each node.
  ○ A full mesh has direct connections between each node.
  ○ A partial mesh has one node connected to all the others with additional connections between some of the nodes.
● There is no need for a central switch.
  ○ Having no central switch means there is no single point of failure.

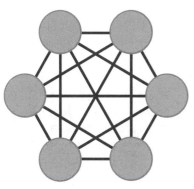
Figure 5.2 A full mesh network layout

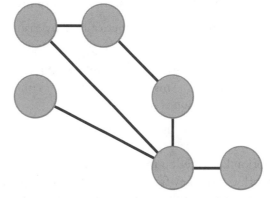
Figure 5.3 A partial mesh network layout

- Data can be sent directly between nodes or can be routed via other nodes.
  - The ability to send signals via multiple paths makes the mesh a very reliable topology.
- The number of connections makes the mesh very expensive and complex to set up.

Exam tip

Networks are often divided into segments that are most likely to be sharing information to minimise traffic. They can still communicate with other segments.

WiFi

WiFi is a technology which uses wireless signals to connect devices.

There are two wavebands in use: 2.4 GHz and 5 GHz.
- 5 GHz has a shorter range than 2.4 GHz.
- 2.4 GHz is close to a range of other uses and is 'crowded' meaning more interference from other devices.
- the range of devices that can use 5 GHz is smaller than that for 2.4 GHz.
- WiFi signals degrade when they pass through solid objects, so the range is limited by any walls or structures in the path of the signal.

Each waveband has multiple **channels** that can used:

> **Channel** A communication link carried by a suitable medium. For WiFi, it is a frequency band within the range available.

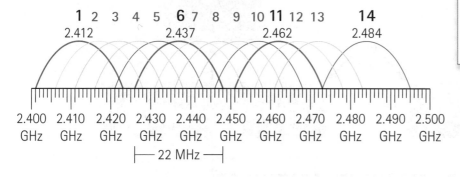

Figure 5.4 A large number of adjacent channels in the 2.4 GHz range

If adjacent channels are in use then there is more chance of interference.

Because channels overlap, only a small number of non-overlapping channels tend to be used.

WiFi signals radiate in all directions and are therefore subject to being intercepted by an enabled device. This makes WiFi more vulnerable than wired technologies and **encryption** is important.

WEP (wireless equivalent privacy) uses static encryption keys for all devices.
- The WEP encryption key is set on the router and on the devices.
- It is possible to work out the key from several intercepted packets.
- People rarely change these because of the inconvenience of resetting all the devices.

WPA (WiFi protected access) scrambles the encryption key using the passphrase and the **SSID (service set identifier)** to generate unique encryption keys for each client.
- These encryption keys are constantly changed.
- WPA2 is an updated version of WPA using more complex algorithms to calculate the encryption key.

> **Encryption** Securing data by applying an encryption key to scramble the data.

> **SSID (service set identifier)** A unique identifier attached to the header of packets sent over a wireless local-area network (WLAN). The SSID acts as a password when a mobile device tries to connect.

Ethernet

REVISED

Ethernet is a common set of technologies used to implement LANs.

Ethernet is most commonly implemented using switches and UTP or fibre-optic cable connections.
- Ethernet typically operates at transmission speeds of up to 100 Gbits per second.
- Data is divided up by the network hardware (NICs and routers) into frames.
- Each frame contains the data plus source and destination MAC addresses.
- The MAC address is a unique identifier allocated to the device at the manufacturing stage that cannot be changed.
- The data is broadcast on the Ethernet network and accepted by the destination device or discarded if that device is not located.

On **TCP/IP** networks the data is divided up into packets by the software.

These packets are then **encapsulated** into frames for sending.

> **TCP/IP** A set of protocols that govern the transfer of data over a network.
>
> **Encapsulation** Enclosing the data inside another data structure to form a single component.
>
> **De-encapsulate** Removing the data from inside an encapsulated item.

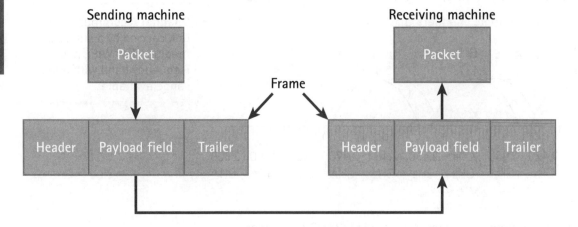

Figure 5.5 Sending and receiving packets

A typical packet contains:

Header
- sender's IP address
- receiver's IP address
- protocol
- packet number
- length of packet

IP address is a unique address allocated to a device by the network.

Protocol is the set of rules used to control how the network communicates.

Payload
- data

Trailer
- end of packet marker
- error correction data

Error correction data is a checksum calculated by the sender and used by the receiver to check if the data has been corrupted. If it has, the receiver will request that the packet be resent.

Packets are used to send data across a network using packet switching.
- The sending device splits the data into packets.
- The router looks at the header and decides which route to send the data on to the receiver.
- The route chosen will depend on other network traffic.
- The packets do not necessarily all follow the same route and may arrive out of sequence.
- The receiver looks at the header and uses the packet number and number of packets to re-assemble the data.

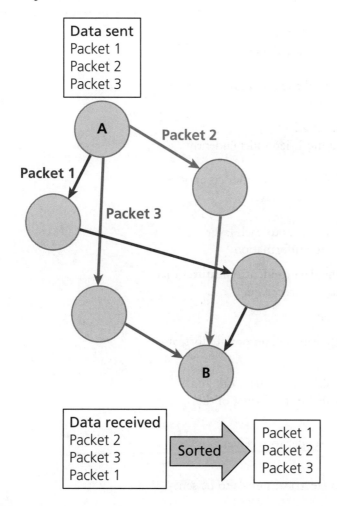

Figure 5.6 Packets of data sent via several routes and reassembled

Exam tip

Ethernet hardware divides data into frames to be transmitted and is sent to all devices in a network segment. Packets are created by software and these packets are then encapsulated by the hardware into frames to be transmitted on the network.

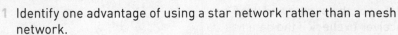

Now test yourself

TESTED

1 Identify one advantage of using a star network rather than a mesh network.
2 Why is it important to set up security on a wireless network?
3 What is the difference between a MAC address and an IP address?

Protocols

REVISED

Internet developers have adopted a set of **protocols** (rules) so that machines from various manufacturers or with various operating systems can communicate with each other.

This set of rules is called TCP/IP (transmission control protocol/internet protocol).

> **Protocol** Set of rules and standards that govern network communication.
>
> **Layering** Rules organised into a distinct order in which they must be applied.

Layers

TCP/IP and many other sets of protocols are **layered**.

● Each layer is a self-contained protocol working independently of the others.
● Each layer is able to take data from the one above and pass it to the one below it.

The advantages of this layering approach are that:

● each protocol layer can be developed and modified independently
● it facilitates modular development
● it reduces the complexity by breaking the task into smaller components
● it enables multiple developers to work on separate layers
● it speeds development
● it forces developers to provide standard interfaces to each layer
● layers are interoperable so they can exchange information.

When data is sent each layer encapsulates the data to identify features that will be required to unpick the original data once received.

There are four layers in the TCP/IP protocol:

Layer 1: Application – making sure the data is in an appropriate format for the application that receives it.

Layer 2: Transport – establishing connections across a network and agreeing the communication rules and details for the format of the packets.

Layer 3: Internet – establishing a path from sender to receiver across different networks.

Layer 4: Network – converting the data to electrical signals to be sent onto the local physical network.

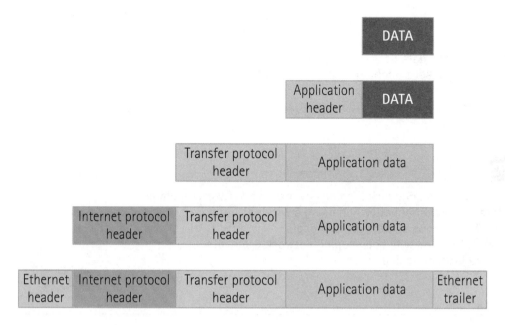

Figure 5.7 Encapsulating data for transmission

Exam tip

It may help you to think of the protocols involved at each layer:
- Layer 1 uses HTTP/FTP etc.
- Layer 2 TCP
- Layer 3 IP
- Layer 4 Ethernet.

Other protocols

HTTP (Hypertext transfer protocol)

Used by web browsers to request and access resources on web servers.

HTTPS (Hypertext transfer protocol secure) is a secure version of HTTP and uses a secure encrypted connection.
- HTTPS provides authentication between the web server and the client to confirm the user is communicating with the correct server (e.g. internet banking or other secure transactions).

FTP (file transfer protocol)

Used to send files from one node to another over the internet. For example, it is used for uploading web pages to a host computer.

POP (post office protocol)

Used to retrieve email from a remote server. It generally moves the email from the server to the client computer.

IMAP (internet message protocol)

Similar to POP but allows complete management of the remote mailbox.

SMTP (simple mail transfer protocol)

An old standard for sending email messages to a mail server.

Now test yourself

TESTED

4 State four items sent as part of a data packet.
5 What are the key features of packet switching to send information from one device to another?
6 Describe what Layer 1 of the TCP/IP protocol does.

Exam practice

1 Describe one advantage of a mesh network topology over a star network topology.
2 Why do we only use three or four channels when using a wireless network?
3 Describe what is meant by 'layering' in network protocols.
4 Identify two advantages of layering when developing network protocols.
5 Identify two protocols used for managing email.

ONLINE

Summary

You should now have an understanding of the following:

Networks can be constructed using various layouts:

- star: all computers are linked to a central device (switch)
- mesh: all computers have a direct connection to each other with no central device.

Wireless networks use radio signals to transmit data:

- they operate on two frequencies 2.4 GHz and 5 GHz
- each waveband is divided into channels for carrying the data
- overlapping channels can suffer from interference.

Data on a wireless network is easy to intercept so must be encrypted:

- WEP uses a static encryption key
- WPA and WPA2 use an algorithm to create a separate encryption key for each device.

Ethernet is the standard used for connecting devices on a network.

Protocols are communication standards used so devices can communicate with each other.

Layering means sets of protocols can be developed and maintained independently.

Layers need to be able to receive and understand data from the layer above and be able to pass data to the layer below in a form it can understand.

6 System security

Networks have numerous access points and are vulnerable to attacks of one sort or another. This provides lots of opportunities for people to obtain or damage data. This is often referred to as hacking.

Hacking

Hacking is an attempt to get around computer security systems. There are various reasons for doing this:

- Theft:
  - ○ to steal money or saleable information
  - ○ break copyright rules by stealing intellectual property and depriving the owner of some income
  - ○ defrauding individuals or organisations.
- Malice:
  - ○ to damage an individual or organisation
  - ○ to make a political point.
- Fun:
  - ○ to prove it is possible.
- Ethical:
  - ○ to expose security weaknesses so that they can be fixed.

Whatever the reason it is illegal in most countries and can result in a severe penalty, possibly including a jail sentence.

Forms of attack

Malware

Malicious software installed on a computer intended to damage or steal information.

Malware	Description
Virus	A computer program, often hidden inside another program, that reproduces itself and usually causes damage such as deleting files.
Worm	A program that need not be embedded inside another program, that replicates itself and spreads throughout a network.
Trojan horse	A malicious program that the user is tricked into installing by pretending to be useful.
Ransomware	Software that interferes with the operation of the user's computer, for example encrypting the storage, or threatening to, unless a sum of money is paid.
Spyware	Software that gathers information about the user and sends it to the originator. This includes key-loggers that record and send keystrokes such as passwords and other sensitive information.
Rootkits	Malicious software that modifies the operating system to avoid detection.
Back doors	An access channel is opened to allow an outsider to bypass security checks.

Protection against malware

- Use up-to-date anti-malware software.
- Update the operating system regularly to fix vulnerabilities.
- Don't open email attachments unless you are certain they are safe.
- Turn off images in email; malware can be embedded within the image.
- Don't open email from unknown senders.
- Avoid peer-to-peer sharing unless files can be scanned on download.
- Update web browsers to fix vulnerabilities.
- Back up data regularly; just in case.
- AND don't forget a mobile phone is also vulnerable to malware.

> **Exam tip**
>
> Auto-update, which automatically downloads and installs updates to key programs, is one way to ensure all vulnerabilities in the operating system or applications are fixed as soon as the manufacturer becomes aware and provides a solution.

Now test yourself

TESTED

1 What is a virus?
2 What is ransomware?
3 Describe three ways to protect against malware being introduced to a system.

Phishing

A common strategy for obtaining sensitive information.

- Email is sent supposedly from a trusted source, e.g. a bank, eBay, PayPal.
- Email refers to a problem with your account and asks you to click on a link.
- Link then asks for account details.

Some of these phishing emails are very carefully prepared and look very much like real emails from the organisation.

Protection against phishing

- Don't open any links within these emails.
- Delete the email.
- Contact the supposed sender directly to confirm it is not genuine.

---

email

PayPal <crim@badguys.com>
To: example@phoney.co.uk
Today at 4:26 AM

Dear Customer example@phoney.co.uk,
We have limited your access to this account.
You will not be able to send/receive and withdraw any money until we confirm your account.
To resolve this matter, please use the link bellow.
Click the link bellow, log in to your account and follow the steps.
http://www.paypal.co.uk.bkx8bm.ppl-forward.com/uk/home/?account=
EjRtNfXSWMcWZ2bjeIxz9vKP5NLR9aKggERK8j4ZNng=
If your verification link doesn't work, it's possible that it was broken by your email systam.
If the verification link isn't clickable or part of the link is cut off, please copy and paste the entire URL into your browser's address bar and press Enter.
We will respond within 24 hours of receiving your information.
Sincerely,
PayPal.co.uk
==================
15.10.2015

Figure 6.1 Example of a phishing email

Brute force attacks

An attempt to identify a password by trial and error.
- Software generates hundreds of potential passwords and tries them to see which one, if any, works.

Protection against brute force attacks

- Use strong passwords.
- Lock accounts after a number of attempts.

Denial of service attacks (DoS)

An attempt to make a system unusable by flooding it with requests.
- Uses up the available bandwidth to make the service unobtainable.
- Groups of attackers, or a single attacker using malware to infect several computers making them 'zombie' computers, flood the target system with requests.
- Done to extort money from the target organisation or simply to disrupt the organisation.
- DoS attacks on government systems have been linked with cyber terrorism.

Protection against DoS attacks

- Use of 'Captcha' or other techniques to confirm that the user is a real person not a computer program.
- There is no real method for preventing these attacks but **traceback** techniques can often identify the perpetrators after the attack.

Data interception and theft

Network data is intercepted.
- Packet sniffing is used to intercept packets and select those of interest.
- A network switch may be configured to send all data to a specific IP address where it can be examined.
- Wireless communications are particularly vulnerable to this.

Protection against data interception

Protecting against these attacks is very difficult since the intruder simply listens to all of the network traffic without disrupting it.
- Strong encryption of the data will make the data useless.
- Packet sniffing can be used by the organisation to monitor the network traffic and identify intrusion attempts.

SQL injection

Many database servers store huge enterprise-wide databases for a business. These will be queried using SQL (structured query language).

By entering SQL queries instead of the data in an online form, the actual SQL can be modified to do something it was not intended to do.

Captcha A type of challenge-response test used in computing to determine whether or not the user is human.

Traceback A method to determine the originator by tracing back through the route taken by a packet to its original IP.

A simple example is the following SQL statement on a server script to retrieve user details:

```
txtSQL = "SELECT * FROM Users WHERE UserId
= " + txtUserId;
```

The intention of this statement is to retrieve all the data (* is a wildcard that means 'everything') from a table called 'Users', where the user ID is data that was input onto an enquiry form. It is put into the variable txtUserId and added to the SQL statement.

So, if a user enters data into a web form such as '150' the SQL will retrieve everything about user 150.

If a user enters 150 OR 1=1, the server interprets this into an SQL statement like this:

```
SELECT * FROM Users WHERE UserId = 150 OR 1=1
```

Now, 1=1 is TRUE, so the SQL will retrieve everything from everyone.

Protecting against SQL injection

Suitable validation techniques on the queries will usually detect this sort of attack. Vulnerabilities are introduced through the lack of thorough validation of data input.

Network policy

Often network vulnerabilities are because of the people using the system not adhering to the proper procedures.

Network managers will devise clear security policies to help users maintain safe working practices.

A security policy must be simple to follow and include:
- what: what needs to be done
- how: how the policies are to be implemented
- why: the reason for the policy
- when: when things should be done
- who: who does what.

A typical security policy will include advice on:
- acceptable use of email and the web
- password management, security, updating frequency and password strength.

The aim of the security policy is to modify employee behaviour towards minimising risks.

Now test yourself

TESTED

4 What is a denial of service attack?
5 What is phishing?
6 Identify two ways to protect yourself from a phishing attack.

Identifying and preventing vulnerabilities

REVISED

Penetration testing

This involves setting up various attacks on the network to identify vulnerabilities.

It tests the network and staff ability to detect and counteract such threats.

Anti-malware software

This minimises the danger from malicious software being introduced onto the system.

- It looks for known malware and identifies suspicious patterns and features associated with malware.
- It scans the hard drive for malware and removes it.
- It scans any incoming files to detect malware and prevent it being introduced.

Exam tip

Remember unless the anti-malware software is up to date, it may not identify security threats.

If the computer has anti-malware software, the software needs to be running to prevent security risks.

Simply installing anti-malware software is not enough.

Firewalls

Firewalls are either software or hardware or both placed between the network (or node) and other networks (or nodes) to control what comes in and what goes out.

- Firewalls are the principle defence against denial of service attacks.
- Packet-filter firewalls inspect each packet and assess it against certain characteristics. They allow it to pass or drop it if not acceptable.
- Firewalls can make decisions based on:
  - the IP address of the sender
  - the protocol used (e.g. blocking FTP).

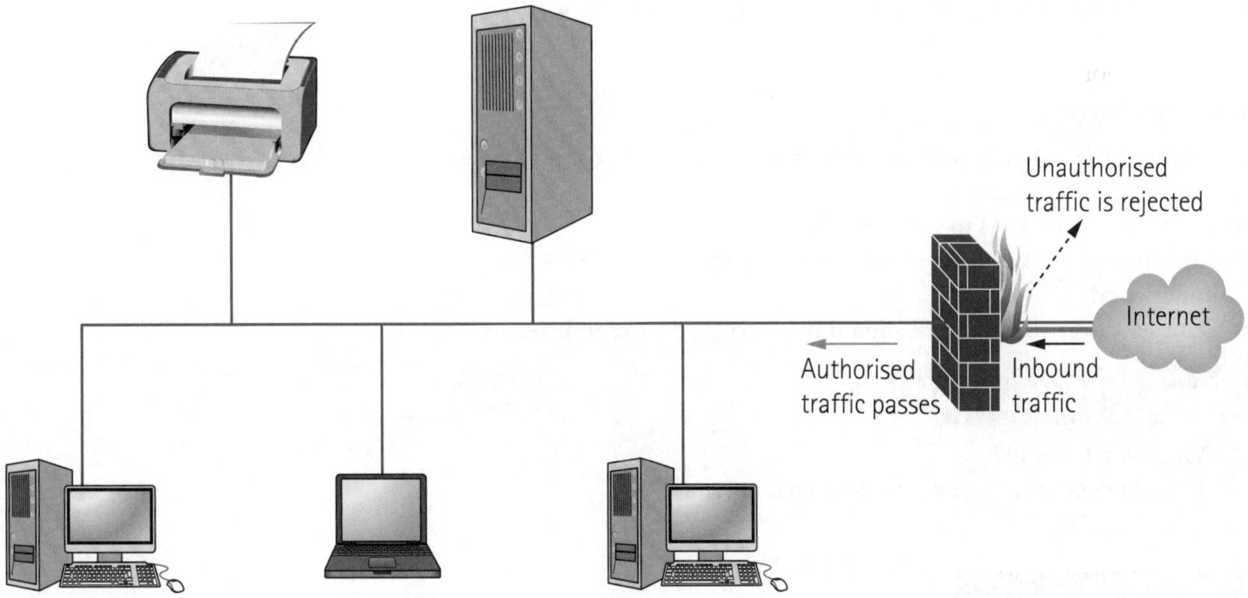

Figure 6.2 A firewall allows authorised traffic but denies access to unauthorised traffic

User access levels

In an organisation, different users need access to different parts of the system so different user access rights can be allocated to individual users or groups of users.

- Users may be granted access to certain files or access to a limited range of files.
- Users may be granted full access (e.g. read/write/delete) or perhaps just read access to files.

Passwords

Passwords are the first line of defence to prevent unauthorised access to a network.

- Passwords should be strong, e.g. including lower case, upper case, numbers and special symbols.
- Passwords should be changed regularly.
- Passwords must not be written down or shared.

Test Your Password		Minimum Requirements
Password:	Ab6$//mmg	• Minimum 8 characters in length
Hide:	☐	• Contains 3/4 of the following items:
Score:	95%	- Uppercase Letters - Lowercase Letters
Complexity:	Very Strong	- Numbers - Symbols

Figure 6.3 **This password is very strong and would be more difficult to crack**

Encryption

Encrypting the data can prevent an outsider making use of the data even if they manage to access it.

- Encryption uses keys to scramble the data.
- The encryption key is required to decrypt the data so that it can be understood.
- Data sent over the network should be encrypted to keep it secure.

Now test yourself

TESTED

7 What is a firewall?
8 How does encryption secure data on a network?

Exam practice

1 Describe what anti-malware software is and how it prevents damage or loss of data on a computer system.
2 Describe two ways an organisation can protect data on its system from unauthorised access.
3 Describe two items of advice to employees that would be included in a network security policy.

ONLINE

Summary

You should now have an understanding of the following:

- Malware is malicious software designed to steal or damage information on a computer system.
- Phishing is an attempt to get sensitive information using fake emails pretending to be from reputable organisations.
- Brute force attacks are attempts to find a password using trial and error.
- Denial of service attacks flood the target system with requests in an attempt to make it unusable.
- Data interception is an attempt to divert data so that it can be intercepted and read.
- SQL injection takes advantage of poor validation to insert an SQL command to return data from an internet database.
- Network security policies are used to advise users on best practice to minimise security threats to the system.
- Penetration testing is an attempt to identify vulnerabilities so that they can be fixed.
- Anti-malware software scans files and drives to identify suspicious software so that it can be removed.
- A firewall sits between the system and the outside to control what comes in and what goes out.
- Passwords are the first line of defence against unauthorised access to a system.
- Encryption uses keys to scramble data so that if data is stolen it is not readable without the correct decryption key.

7 System software

System software sits between the hardware and the applications and provides the operating system and essential utilities required to make the computer usable.

Operating systems

REVISED

Operating systems are collections of programs that tell the hardware what to do.

They are necessary on computer systems ranging from mobile phones and video consoles to large supercomputers and:
- provide a user interface
- provide an interface between the running programs and the computer hardware
- manage the computer hardware and peripherals
- manage programs installed and running
- manage data transfer between memory locations, the CPU and secondary storage
- provide a file system for storing and retrieving files
- manage security and organising data so that it is not overwritten.

User interface

The user interface allows the user to interact with the computer.

Command line

- Text-based interface suited to technical users.
- Commands are typed directly in the command line.
- Provides for single powerful commands to manage the system efficiently.
- Sequences of commands can be combined into a program called a shell script (batch file) so that single commands can cause multiple actions.

> **Command line** Where text-based commands can be given to the operating system.

```
[GEORGEs-iMac:~ george2$ ls
Accellion              Dropbox              Public
Applications           Ephox                hello.sh
Desktop                FW_ AMEC.rtfd        mysql
Documents              Google Drive         records.txt
Downloads              Library              scores.txt
Downloads-1.(null)     Movies               weightwatch.csv
Downloads-2.(null)     Music                weightwatch.txt
Downloads-3.(null)     Pictures             words.txt
[GEORGEs-iMac:~ george2$ cd documents
[GEORGEs-iMac:documents george2$ cd piresources
[GEORGEs-iMac:piresources george2$ ls
 125292-raspberry-pi-resources-link.pdf
 125296-classroom-challenge-architecture-learner-sheet.pdf
 125297-classroom-challenge-architecture-teacher-sheet.pdf
 125299-classroom-challenge-connecting-to-a-network-learner-sheet.pdf
 125300-classroom-challenge-connecting-to-a-network-teacher-sheet.pdf
 125301-classroom-challenge-simple-animation-learner-sheet.pdf
 125303-classroom-challenge-simple-animation-teacher-sheet.pdf
 GEORGEs-iMac:piresources george2$
```

Figure 7.1 Unix commands on an Apple Mac; the commands used are ls (list) and cd (change directory)

This simple shell script, called hello.sh, asks for a name then says: hello, 'name', nice to meet you.

```
#!/bin/sh
printf "What is your name? ->"
read NAME
echo "Hello, $NAME, nice to meet you"
```

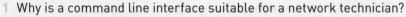

```
Last login: Mon Jan 18 12:02:48 on ttys000
[GEORGEs-iMac:~ george2$ ./hello.sh
What is your name? -> Fred
Hello, Fred, nice to meet you
GEORGEs-iMac:~ george2$ █
```

Figure 7.2 Shell script running

Graphical user interface (GUI)

The most common type of interface found on most personal computers and devices.

● Icons (small pictures) are used to represent **applications** and actions.
● Using icons removes the need to learn commands.
● Particularly suited to touchscreen devices such as mobile phones and tablets.

Voice input

Voice recognition technology is widely in use on mobile phones and in call centres where quite complex information can be provided simply by speaking into the telephone.

Application A program designed for a specific purpose.

Figure 7.3 A smartphone showing its GUI

Now test yourself

TESTED ☐

1 Why is a command line interface suitable for a network technician?
2 What features of a GUI make it appropriate to a non-specialist computer user?
3 Why do call some centres use voice interfaces when dealing with customer queries?

Memory management

Managing the available memory is one of the key tasks for the operating system.

● Several programs will be in memory at the same time.
● Each program will have its own data and the operating system makes sure that this is not modified by another program.
● As programs complete and others start, the operating system is responsible for allocating the free memory to programs.

Figure 7.4 Voice input on a mobile phone

Multi-tasking

Several programs are often run apparently at the same time; this is called multi-tasking.

- The operating system keeps the CPU as busy as possible to get the most out of the computer system.
- If the current program is waiting, e.g. loading or writing data to secondary storage, the operating system will load another program to the CPU.
- End users do not notice programs stopping and starting because it happens very quickly
- The CPU time is divided between processes by the operating system, which allocates time based on priorities to make sure the system operates as efficiently as possible. This is known as **scheduling**.

> **Scheduling** The process of arranging, controlling and optimising work and workloads.

File management

The computer stores data on secondary storage in files.

- The operating system is responsible for storing and retrieving these files.
- The operating system provides facilities to manage these files, e.g. moving, deleting, renaming etc.
- The operating system manages the secondary storage, dividing it up into identifiable areas so that the location of each file can be stored in an index.
- Storage is usually organised on a hierarchical basis.

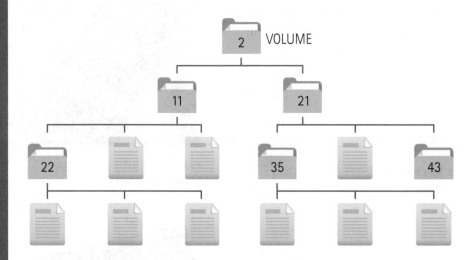

Figure 7.5 A hierarchical files system

Peripheral management

The operating system manages any **peripheral** devices used to input, output or store data.

- Communication with peripheral devices is controlled by signals produced by device drivers.
- Device drivers are software utilities provided by the manufacturer that communicate with the operating system and the peripheral device.
- Different operating systems will require different device drivers.

> **Peripheral** A device connected to a computer system such as a printer, a mouse or a keyboard

- Device drivers are regularly updated by the manufacturer to improve performance or fix bugs.
- Most device drivers allow the user to make minor modifications to the way a peripheral behaves by changing settings.
- Device drivers take care of the peripheral so that application programmers do not need to concern themselves with the details of any devices that may be used.

> **Exam tip**
>
> Device drivers sit between the device and the operating system. The drivers need to be able to communicate with both so that there is no direct interaction between the operating system and the device. This is an example of layering.

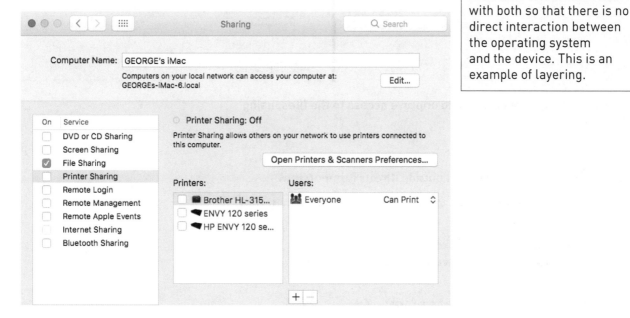

Figure 7.6 Managing print sharing

User management

A typical computer system will have more than one user. These users can be allocated their own accounts, security and individual settings with different access rights to programs and files.

Now test yourself

TESTED

4 Describe two tasks carried out by an operating system.
5 Why might you need different access settings for users both using the same computer?

Utility software

REVISED

Defragmentation

As files are written to and removed from secondary storage, the contents become fragmented, with segments of files scattered throughout the disk.

This happens because files are all different sizes, leaving gaps of various sizes.

Over time, this leads to large files being stored in multiple locations on the disk.

Since the read/write head has to move between these fragments, it makes access to files considerably slower.

Defragmentation software reorganises the files on the disk, reuniting fragmented files and putting free spaces together.

> **Utility** A small program designed to carry out a limited maintenance task.

> **Defragmentation** Software that brings together fragments of files and free space on a disk.

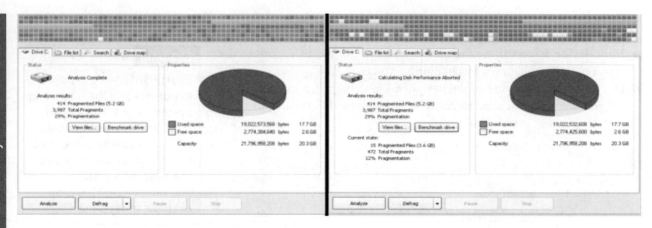

Figure 7.7 Defragmenting a disk to improve access to the files, using Defraggler®

Encryption software

Securing data on a computer from outside threats is important.

Data can be encrypted to prevent anyone from reading the data if they have managed to access it.

Encryption uses keys, or a pair of keys, with an algorithm that scrambles the data so that it cannot be read without the appropriate key.

Figure 7.8 Adding encryption to a folder on the hard disk drive

Compression software

- Enables data to be compressed into a smaller file by removing redundant data.
- It is supplied with a number of operating systems to save on disk space (though this is no longer necessary given the availability of low-cost large secondary-storage devices)
- It is used for large files that need to be moved to smaller media or transmitted electronically.

Now test yourself

TESTED

6 Describe two utility programs commonly found on personal computers.

Backup

Data stored on the main secondary storage in a computer is potentially at risk of loss or damage. It is important that this data is backed up.

A **backup** is a copy of the files on a computer so that the system can be restored if the data is damaged or lost.

Options for backing up data include:
- backing up important files
- backing up the whole drive
- using an external device such as a flash drive or external hard disk
- using a remote data storage service, a cloud server.

> **Backup** A copy of the data on a drive used to restore them if they are lost or damaged.

Full backup

All files on the drive are copied every time a backup happens.

Advantages	Disadvantages
Able to restore data faster than other methods.	Slowest method of backup.
Only requires the last backup to restore all the data.	Requires most storage space.
	Inefficient with lots of duplicated data stored.

Incremental backup

Uses an initial full backup, then regular backups for those files that have changed.

Advantages	Disadvantages
Able to back up faster than full backup.	Slowest restore.
Requires less space.	Needs the full backup plus all the incremental backups to restore all the data.
Does not store any duplicated files.	

Figure 7.9 Apple Time Machine backup and restore facility

Exam practice

1 Explain what defragmentation is and why it might be needed.
2 Compare the advantages and disadvantages of incremental backup over full backup.
3 Explain multi-tasking.

ONLINE

Summary

You should now have an understanding of the following:

Operating systems:
- help to control the hardware
- provide facilities for other software to run
- manage the file handling
- provide a user interface
- manage security
- manage memory.

Multi-tasking is the apparent ability to run several programs simultaneously.
- The CPU switches between programs very quickly so that user is unaware of the programs stopping and starting.

The operating system manages multiple users for a computer, allocating each one their own accounts, security and settings.

Utility software performs maintenance tasks:
- device drivers are utility programs that manage peripheral devices
- defragmenters are utility programs that are used to tidy up disk drives by bringing together fragments of programs and free space.

Backups can be full, backing up all the files every time, or incremental, backing up all the files once and then any changes.

8 Ethical, legal, cultural and environmental issues

The widespread use of computer technology in all aspects of daily life has brought many benefits for the individual and society.

Alongside the benefits, the widespread use of computer technology has also generated several problems, from computer crime to issues with the freedom of the individual.

The fact that we depend upon computer technology in so many parts of our daily lives brings a reliance on technology that makes us all more vulnerable to these problems.

Legal issues

Computer crime consists of a wide range of existing and new criminal activities including:
- unauthorised access to data and computer systems for the purpose of theft or damage
- identity theft
- software piracy
- fraud
- harassment, such as trolling.

Many of these activities are criminalised by Acts of Parliament.

The Data Protection Act (1998)

The control of stored data about an individual, and the rights of the individual to access, check and correct this data.

There are eight provisions in the Data Protection Act:
1 Data should be processed fairly and lawfully (i.e. the data must not be obtained by deception and the purpose for the data being collected should be revealed to the data subject).
2 Data should only be used for the purpose specified to the data protection agency and should not be disclosed to other parties without the necessary permission.
3 Data should be relevant and not excessive.
4 Data should be accurate and up to date.
5 Data should only be kept for as long as necessary.
6 Individuals have the right to access data kept about them and should be able to check and update the data if necessary.
7 Security must be in place to prevent unauthorised access to the data.
8 Data may not be transferred outside the EU unless the country has adequate data protection legislation.

The data controller in an organisation is responsible for the accuracy and security of data kept about the data subject.

There are some exemptions to the data protection act principles.
- National security: any data processed in relation to national security is exempt from the Act.
- Crime and taxation: any data used to detect or prevent crime or to assist with the collection of taxes is exempt from the Act.

- Domestic purposes: any data used solely for individual, family or household use is exempt from the Act.

Computer Misuse Act (1990)

It is a criminal offence to make any unauthorised access to computer material with the intent to:
- commit further offences (e.g. hacking)
- modify the computer material (e.g. distributing malware).

Features used to minimise these threats include:
- digital signatures or certificates that use encrypted messages to confirm the identity of the sender
- SSL (secure socket layer), a protocol that enables encrypted links between computers to ensure the security of a transaction
- user IDs, passwords and access rights, which are used for basic identification of users and their legitimate rights to access specific data
- anti-malware software such as anti-virus and anti-spyware applications for identifying and removing suspicious software on a computer system
- firewalls.

Copyright Designs and Patents Act (1988)

Protects the intellectual property of an individual or organisation.

It is illegal to copy, modify or distribute software or other intellectual property without the relevant permission.

This includes video and audio where peer-to-peer streaming has had a significant impact on the income of the copyright owners.

Most software will be issued with a license explaining what can and cannot be done with the software, including copying and distributing.

Creative Commons licensing

An organisation that issues licences allowing the user to modify or distribute parts of the software under certain conditions.

Also known as 'some rights reserved'.

Open-source and proprietary software

Software developed under open standards has the source code available:
- Developed and updated by a community of programmers
- Can be installed on as many computers as necessary
- Others can modify the code and distribute it
- Versions are made available at no or very little cost
- Relies upon the community for testing and support, modified versions may not be supported or fully tested.

Proprietary software is written by organisations trying to make a profit.
- Source code is kept securely and versions of the software are distributed as executable programs so that the user is not able to access the source code or modify it.
- Software is copyright protected making it illegal to modify or distribute it.
- Usually licensed for a fixed number of computer systems.
- Software is fully tested and supported by the organisation.

Freedom of Information Act (2000)

This provides the public with the right access to information held by public authorities.

- This Act covers any recorded information held by public bodies, for example government departments, local authorities, state schools and the police.
- Public authorities are obliged to publish certain data about what they do.
- Members of the public can request information about the activities of public bodies.
- Journalists often use this act to scrutinise the activities of public authorities.

Now test yourself

TESTED

1 What data is exempt from the Data Protection Act?
2 Under which Act can a member of the public obtain information about the work of a local council?
3 Which Act makes it illegal to distribute a virus?

Exam tip

These questions may well be asked within a wider context so make sure your answers reflect this rather than simply rewriting the bullet points.

Ethical issues

REVISED

Ethics is about what society considers right or wrong. This is to some extent a personal matter, but organisations such as the British Computer Society (BCS) have some ethical standards they believe computing professionals should adhere to.

Privacy

Most people agree they have a right to some degree of privacy.

- We provide lots of personal information to organisations on the internet when we set up accounts.
- Organisations often ask for the right to share this information when people sign up for an account.
- Personal details and details of activities are often shared on social media.

CCTV cameras in public places to monitor behaviour:

Advantages	Disadvantages
Security footage that can be used to solve crimes and keep us safe on the streets.	A 'big brother' approach, constantly tracking what we do and where we go.

Mobile phone signals can be tracked:

Advantages	Disadvantages
Useful for finding friends.	When we take a picture, the location and time are recorded.
Can provide valuable evidence for the police.	Images we might not want to share are often saved in the cloud, making them available to hackers.

Workplace logging; activities and the use of computers and phones:

Advantages	Disadvantages
Enables the employer to monitor the effectiveness of an employee.	Intrusion into the life of the employee.
Provides insight into working patterns.	Constant pressure to perform at work.
Can reduce the risk of employees using the organisations facilities for illegal or unacceptable purposes .	Monitoring social media posts.

Social media provides an excellent way to make and keep in contact with other people:

Advantages	Disadvantages
Sharing recent activities can keep people up to date with what you like and what you are doing.	Trolling and cyber bullying are attempts to cause someone distress by posting insulting or threatening messages and can be very unpleasant.
	Unguarded comments or inappropriate images posted on social media are available to a wide audience and may be seen by family, friends, work colleagues or employers.

Cultural issues

REVISED

Stakeholders

Stakeholders are those who have an interest in the situation.

Whether something is a positive or a negative does depend on the viewpoint of the stakeholder.

Censorship and the internet

This is the deliberate suppression by an organisation or government of:
● socially unacceptable material
● what they regard as dangerous information.

Access to websites is controlled by 'blacklist' of unacceptable sites, 'whitelists' which identify all acceptable sites and block anything else, and through dynamic examination of the websites for unacceptable material.

To what extent the internet is censored varies from organisation to organisation and from country to country. Governments often take differing views about what is acceptable and what is not.

The debate is about where to draw the line between protecting the public and infringing their rights to free speech and access to information.

Computers in the workforce

Computers are used throughout the workforce which has, in many cases, changed the skill set required, for example:
● robots making cars: instead of a welder to make the cars we now require a technician to maintain the robots
● online shopping: instead of a shop assistant we now use automated warehouses with workers collecting and packing objects

> **Exam tip**
>
> When answering questions, be careful to note the point of view you are expected to take when looking at an issue. A positive point from one point of view may be a negative one from another.

● online banking: we now use automated telephone systems and no longer need as many high street banks and the associated workforce.

Figure 8.1 Robots building a car

Computer systems are also used extensively to make decisions, for example:
● plant automation that constantly monitors and responds to complex and dangerous processes, e.g. chemical plants
● stock market trading where the system can respond rapidly to any changes
● airborne collision avoidance systems that monitor all aircraft in the vicinity and can take immediate action to avoid a collision
● credit-card checking looks for unusual patterns in use to identify potentially fraudulent activity.

Many organisations collect data about individuals, for example:
● searches on the internet and social media are monitored and analysed to focus advertising for an individual
● social media, financial, shared contacts, travel and search history details are monitored to track criminal or terrorist activity
● medical data is collected and analysed to develop new treatments for various conditions.

> **Exam tip**
>
> These topics are often asked as level of response questions expecting a balanced argument. Think about both sides of the issue, present the evidence for both sides and reach a conclusion based on the evidence.

Now test yourself

TESTED

4 Identify two advantages of monitoring an employee's use of the internet for an organisation.
5 Why are computers used to make automatic decisions as part of a collision avoidance system on an airplane?

Environmental issues

REVISED

Most modern computers consume low levels of electricity but are often left running permanently with data centres accounting for around two per cent of all energy used on the planet, the same as air travel.

As with all consumer electronics, computers use up valuable resources and their disposal raises environmental issues.

A lot of energy and non-renewable resources are used when making a computer.

Computers are made from some pretty toxic material including airborne dioxins, polychlorinated biphenyls (PCBs), cadmium, chromium, radioactive isotopes and mercury.

● These materials need to be handled with great care when disposing of computer equipment.
● Old computer equipment is often shipped off to countries with lower environmental standards to reduce the cost of disposal.
● In some cases, children pick over the waste to extract metals that can be recycled and sold thus exposing them to significant danger.

Figure 8.2 Picking over discarded computer equipment to extract metals

Exam practice

1 What are the provisions in the Data Protection Act that relate to the storage of data by an organisation?
2 Describe Creative Commons.
3 Describe one advantage and one disadvantage of data capture by an organisation for the individual.

ONLINE

Summary

You should now have an understanding of the following:

● The Data Protection Act refers to the rights of the individual and the responsibilities of the organisation regarding storage of personal data.
● The Computer Misuse Act makes unauthorised access illegal. This Act makes hacking and the distribution of malware a criminal offence.
● The Copyrights, Designs and Patents Act protects individual intellectual property. This Act refers to making illegal copies of software, music, films and other intellectual property.
● Creative Commons issues licences that allow the user to modify, copy and distribute parts

of the software under certain circumstances, 'some rights reserved'.
● Open-source software is created and maintained by a community. The source code is freely available. It is often low cost or even no cost software.
● Proprietary software is created and maintained by an organisation for profit. The source code is not available. It always has an associated cost.
● The viewpoint of the stakeholder will change how ethical, social, cultural and environmental issues are seen.

Topic 2
Computational thinking, algorithms and programming

9 Algorithms

Computational thinking

Computational thinking is a problem-solving method that involves the application of thought processes to open-ended problems.

Computational thinking uses several processes to help us solve complex problems.

Abstraction

This involves taking a real-life situation and creating a model of it so that it can be analysed.

Using a model with symbols, we can identify the important aspects of the problem and ignore the unnecessary detail.

Examples of **abstraction**:
- variables in a program represent real values
- functions in a program to represent a group of actions that produce a result
- maps are a representation of part of the Earth's surface.

> **Abstraction** Making a model of a situation so that it can be analysed.

Decomposition

Decomposition means breaking the complex problem down into smaller parts.
- Dealing with each small part of the problem is much simpler than trying to deal with the complex problem.
- Breaking the problem down into several sub-problems allows us to work on each of these individually and then combine them into a solution to the complex problem.
- For very large problems, a team of programmers can work on individual parts of the problem to achieve a solution.

> **Decomposition** Breaking a problem down into sub-problems.

Algorithmic thinking

An **algorithm** is a method of defining a solution to a problem; it is a series of steps that solve a problem.

An algorithm that solves a problem can be the basis for a solution to a similar problem.
- Looking for patterns in problems can identify existing solutions to similar problems that can be adapted for the current one.

> **Algorithms** A set of steps that describe a solution to a problem.

Expressing algorithms

Flowcharts or pseudocode can be used to express an algorithm.

Pseudocode is a structured form of language that approximates to program code but without the programming language details.

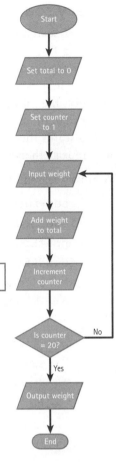

Example

Here is an example of pseudocode. It is not any particular version of pseudocode but it is clear enough to follow.

```
Set total to zero
Set counter to one
While counter is less than or equal to twenty
  Input the next weight
  Add the weight into the total
  Add 1 to counter
  Set the average weight to the total divided by
  twenty
Print the average weight
```

Standard searching algorithms

REVISED

Linear search

This looks at each item in turn until it finds the target or until it reaches the end of the list.

A linear search expressed in pseudocode:

```
position=0
len=lengthoflist
while position<len AND
list[position]!=itemsearchedfor
  add 1 to position
endwhile
if position>=len then
  print("item not found")
else
  print("item found at position"+position)
endif
```

Figure 9.1 The same algorithm expressed in a flowchart

Example

For the list:

position	0	1	2	3
item	Hat	Coat	Gloves	Shoes
	↑	↑	↑	

Searching for Gloves, the algorithm will look at positions 0, 1 then 2.

It will return "Item found at position 2".

Binary search

A binary search requires all the data to be ordered before it can search for an item:

- it first looks at the midpoint of the list
- if the item is found it reports it
- if not, then it decides if the item it is looking for is earlier or later in the list than the midpoint.
- it discards the half of the list not containing the item
- it repeats the process with this new list.

A binary search expressed in pseudocode:

```
item=input("enter the item wanted")
lowerbound =0
upperbound=lengthoflist-1
found=false
while found==false AND lowerbound!=upperbound
    midpoint=round((lowerbound+upperbound)/2)
    if list[midpoint]==item then
        found=true
    elseif list[midpoint]<item then
        lowerbound=midpoint+1
    else
        upperbound=midpoint-1
    endif
endwhile
if found==true then
    print("item found at"+midpoint)
else
    print("item not present")
endif
```

- Binary searches will halve the amount of data left in the list at each iteration.
- Linear searches check each item in turn.
- The binary search is generally faster for an ordered list.

Exam tip

Note: a binary search requires an ordered list but linear search can find an item in an unordered list.

Now test yourself

TESTED ☐

1 In computational thinking terms, what is the London Underground map an example of?
2 What is decomposition?
3 Which of linear or binary search would be appropriate for finding T in the list D, J, A, B, T, R, K, M?

Example

For the list:

position	0	1	2	3	4	5	6
item	A	B	C	D	E	F	G

Searching for C:

position	0		1	2	3		4	5	6
item	A		B	C	D		E	F	G
	Lower bound				Mid point				Upper bound

C in lower half of the list so we discard the top half.

position	0	1	2
item	A	B	C
	Lower bound	Mid point	Upper bound

C is later in the list than the midpoint so we discard the lower section of the list.

position	2
item	C

We have now found the target value at position 2.

Standard sorting algorithms

Bubble sort

A bubble sort is the easiest sort algorithm to understand but it is very inefficient.

- Start at the beginning of the list and compare the first two items.
- If they are in order, fine.
- If not swap them over and record the fact that a swap has been made.
- Now look at the next pair, the second and third items.
- Repeat this procedure until you get to the end of the list.
- If you have made a swap then start again at the beginning.
- Repeat this until you do not make a swap on a complete pass through the list.

```
swapflag = true
while swapflag == true
  swapflag = false
  position = 0
  for position = 0 to listlength - 2
    compare the items at current position and
    position + 1
    if out of order swap them and set swapflag
    to true
  next position
endwhile
```

Example

For the list:

0	1	2	3	4
D	A	C	B	E

D	A	C	B	E	D and A not in order swap and set flag to true
A	D	C	B	E	D and C not in order so swap, flag is true
A	C	D	B	E	D and B not in order so swap, flag is true
A	C	B	D	E	D and E in order no action
A	C	B	D	E	Swapflag is true so set to false and start again
A	C	B	D	E	A and C in order no action, flag is false
A	C	B	D	E	C and B not in order, swap and set flag to true
A	B	C	D	E	C and D in order, no action flag is true
A	B	C	D	E	D and E in order, no action flag is true
A	B	C	D	E	Swapflag is true so start again, set flag to false

Since the data is in order there will be no swaps on the next pass.

The flag will remain false throughout the next pass and the algorithm will stop.

Advantages	Disadvantages
Bubble sort is easy to program.	Takes many steps to complete the process, even for a small list.
	Is inefficient and not suited to large lists.

Merge sort

If we have two sorted lists we can merge them into a single sorted list by
- comparing the first item in each list
- removing the one that comes first when sorted and add to a new list
- repeating until one list is empty
- adding the remaining items in the non-empty list to the new list.

The pseudocode for merging sorted lists:

```
while list1 is not empty AND list2 is not empty
   if the first item in list1<list2 then
      remove the first item from list1 and add it to newlist
   else
      remove the first item from list2 and add it to newlist
   endif
endwhile
if list1 is empty then
   add the remainder of list2 to newlist
else
   add the remainder of list1 to newlist
endif
```

Example

For the two lists:

List1	List2
3,5	4,8,9,11

Compare 3 and 4. 3 is the smallest so it is removed from List1 and placed in Newlist.

Newlist	List1	List2
3	5	4,8,9,11

Now we compare 5 and 4. 4 is removed and placed in Newlist.

Newlist	List1	List2
3,4	5	8,9,11

We repeat until one list is empty.

Newlist
3,4,5

Now List1 is empty we append the contents of List2 to Newlist.

Newlist
3,4,5,8,9,11

If we start from an unordered list we can create a set of ordered lists by having just one item per list.

By merging these one-item lists into two-item, then four-item lists etc. we will eventually sort the data in the list.

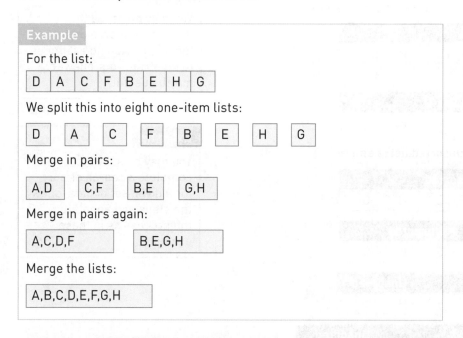

Example

For the list:

| D | A | C | F | B | E | H | G |

We split this into eight one-item lists:

| D | | A | | C | | F | | B | | E | | H | | G |

Merge in pairs:

| A,D | | C,F | | B,E | | G,H |

Merge in pairs again:

| A,C,D,F | | B,E,G,H |

Merge the lists:

| A,B,C,D,E,F,G,H |

Advantages	Disadvantages
Merge sort is more efficient than the bubble sort.	Is slow for small lists.
Takes the same time for any list regardless of how unordered it is.	Takes up a lot of memory creating so many lists.

Insertion sort

The insertion sort takes an item from the unsorted list and places it in the correct position in a sorted list.

The pseudocode for an insertion sort is:

```
make the first item the sorted list and the
remaining items are the unsorted list.

while there are items remaining in the unsorted
list

    take the first item from the unsorted list.
    while there is an item in the sorted list
    which is smaller
    than itself
       swap with  that item
    endwhile
endwhile
```

Example

For the unordered list:

Unsorted list							
D	A	C	F	B	E	H	G

Make the first item a sorted list:

Sorted	Unsorted list						
D	A	C	F	B	E	H	G

Take the first item in the unsorted list, A, and insert it into the sorted list.

A comes before D so it is inserted before D in the sorted list:

Sorted		Unsorted list					
A	D	C	F	B	E	H	G

C comes after A but before D:

Sorted list			Unsorted list				
A	C	D	F	B	E	H	G

Repeat this process until the unsorted list is empty.

Sorted list				Unsorted			
A	C	D	F	B	E	H	G

Sorted list					Unsorted		
A	B	C	D	F	E	H	G

Sorted list						Unsorted	
A	B	C	D	E	F	H	G

Sorted list							Unsorted
A	B	C	D	E	F	H	G

Sorted list							
A	B	C	D	E	F	G	H

Exam tip

You are expected to be aware of the advantages and disadvantages of the different searching and sorting algorithms for a given situation.

Exam tip

You may be asked to describe a search or sort technique. Adding examples to illustrate your answer may be useful.

Exam tip

You may be asked to complete a search or sort for a given set of data, show the steps and annotate the process as in these examples.

Advantages	Disadvantages
Insertion sort is easy to code.	Not very efficient with large lists.
Is good for small lists.	
Doesn't use a great deal of memory compared to the merge sort.	
Quick to check if a list is already sorted unlike the merge sort.	

Now test yourself

4 Why might a merge sort be problematic for a set of data with several thousand items in it?
5 Which sort would you use to check if a set of data was in order?
6 Which of the three sort techniques above would you choose for a large set of data?

Writing algorithms

REVISED

Algorithms are used to express a solution to a problem and are the basis for a coded solution.

The first step in the process is to decompose the problem into smaller sub-problems that can be expressed in as a series of steps.

For example, a program to check the strength of a password can be described by this series of steps:
● read each character of the password
● if it is uppercase set upper flag to true
● if it is lowercase set lower flag to true
● if it is a symbol set symbol flag to true
● if all three flags are set then return 'Strong'
● if two flags are set return 'Medium'
● otherwise return 'Weak'.

This is an algorithm that describes a solution method but it does not identify the programming steps required.

A better pseudocode algorithm will include the steps required when coding the solution.

```
initialise upper, lower and symbol to 0
input password
for i= 1 to len(password)
   if char(i,password) is uppercase then upper=1
   elif char(i,password) is lowercase then lower=1
   elif char(i,password) is symbol then symbol=1
   endif
next i
strength = upper+lower+symbol
if strength == 3 then
   print "Strong"
elif strength == 2 then
   print "Medium"
else
   print "Weak"
endif
```

Using this pseudocode, each step can be turned into the equivalent code to produce a solution. This is because the structure looks like that for the program it describes.

This does not explain exactly how to code this, for example the syntax for taking a single character from a string or how to check if it is uppercase or lowercase.

Flowcharts

Flowcharts are another method for describing solution. Flowcharts provide a visual representation of the code.

There are some standard shapes that are commonly used.

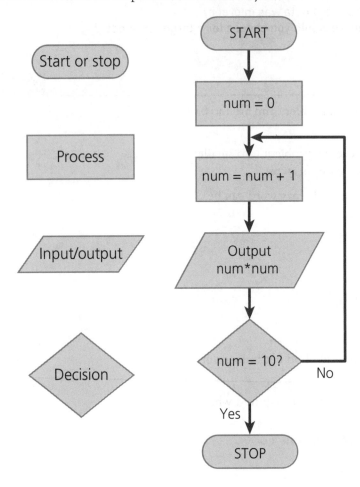

Figure 9.2 The flowchart shows a program to print out the first 10 square numbers

Exam tip

Questions will often ask you to interpret, correct or complete algorithms. Common errors are loops not set correctly.

Exam practice

1 Show the process for finding the item 'M' in this list: A, B, D, E, F, K, L, M, N, P, X using a binary search.
2 Show the process for sorting the list C, D, B, A using:
   (a) bubble sort
   (b) merge sort
   (c) insertion sort
3 There are two errors in the following algorithm to identify what bus fare rate to charge. Identify and correct them.

```
input age
if age<5 then free
elif age >5 AND age >16 then half price
else full fare
endif
```

ONLINE

Summary

You should now have an understanding of the following:
Computational thinking is an approach to problem solving which involves applying thought processes to open-ended problems.
● Decomposition and abstraction are key elements of successful problem solving.

Algorithms can be written as flowcharts or in pseudocode.
● Flowcharts provide a visual interpretation of the solution.
● Pseudocode uses semi-structured language to describe the solution in terms of the processes to be completed.

Linear search techniques can be applied to unordered lists.
● Each element of the list is looked at in turn until the item is found or the end of the list is reached.

Binary search can be used on ordered lists.
● It looks at the midpoint of the list discarding the half of the list without the item.
● It repeats this until the item is found or there is just one item which not the search item.

Bubble sorts are inefficient and compare pairs of items and swapping if not in the right order.

This is repeated for the whole list and if a swap is made during a pass through the list it repeats the process until no swaps are made.
● Easy to program.
● Inefficient even for small lists.

Merge sort splits the list into single item lists, which are merged into ordered new lists.

This process is repeated until all the data is merged into a single ordered list.
● More efficient than the bubble sort.
● Takes the same time for any list regardless of how unordered it is.
● Is slow for small lists.
● Takes up a lot of memory.

Insertion sort uses a single list comparing the first item in an unsorted section with those in a sorted section and inserting the item in the correct position.
● Is good for small lists.
● Doesn't use a great deal of memory.
● Quick to check if a list is already sorted.
● Not very efficient with large lists.

10 Programming techniques

Variables and constants

Variables

Computer programs are an abstraction of reality.

Programs use **variables** to represent real world items.

We see the use of variables in mathematics to represent values.

For example, in the equation:

$F=ma$

F represents force, M represents mass and a represents acceleration.

These are all variables.

Variables are labels we use to represent values stored in computer memory.
● When we declare a variable the computer allocates a location in memory to store any values assigned to that variable.

> **Variable** A label that refers to a memory location containing a value that can be accessed and changed by a program.

Constants

Constants are labels we use to represent fixed values:
● a location in memory is allocated to the label
● the program is not allowed to change the value stored.

If we are using the same equation to refer to the force due to gravity at sea level, the acceleration does not change and we might modify the equation to

$F=mg$

where g is the acceleration due to gravity at sea level, approximately $9.8m/s^2$.

Since the value for g does not change we would declare g as a **constant**.

> **Constant** A label that refers to a memory location containing a value that can be accessed but not changed by a program.

Data types

Data type	Comments	Example
Integer	Whole numbers, such as quantities.	6, 0, -3, 2112
Real (float)	Numbers with a decimal part, such as prices	3.23, -1.05
Boolean	Can only take one of two values, i.e. true or false.	TRUE/FALSE, 1/0, yes/no
Character	A single character from the character set	a , N, @ ,), 6
String	A string of alphanumeric characters, such as names and telephone numbers	Cat, G12&5

Exam practice answers and quick quizzes at **www.hoddereducation.co.uk/myrevisionnotes**

Input and output

A program will generally take an input and process this to provide an output.

Figure 10.1 Input–process–output cycle

A program to calculate the force due to gravity on a mass might be:

```
g=9.8
m=float(input("Mass of object "))
F=m*g
print("force is ",F)
```

- The constant *g* is **declared** with an assigned value.
- A value is input by the user and assigned to the variable *m*.
- The computer uses the values for *m* and *g* to process the data to calculate the force *F*.
- *F* is output by the computer.

Assignment

When data is input or declared it is **assigned** to a variable.

We assign values to variables using the = sign, for example

```
g=9.8, m=float(input("Mass of object")
```

Casting

We use casting to change or set the data type for a variable.
- The input from the user has been **typecast** (cast) as a floating point, or real, number so that it can accept numbers with decimal points.

> **Assignment** Setting the value of a variable or constant.
>
> **Declaration** Identifying a variable or constant so that a suitable memory location can be assigned to it.
>
> **Typecast** Casting a variable to a particular type, e.g. str, int or float.

Arithmetic operators

REVISED

The basic arithmetic operators that can be applied to numeric data are:

Operator	Name	Example	Result
+	Add	3+2	5
–	Subtract	6-2	4
*	Multiply	3*4	12
/	Divide	12/3	4
^	Exponentiation	3^2	9

There are also arithmetic operators that can only be applied to integers:

Operator	Name	Comment	Result
MOD %	Modulus	MOD returns the remainder after division 14/3 = 4 rem **2**	14MOD3 = 2
DIV //	Quotient	DIV returns the whole number part of the division 14/3 = **4** rem 2	14DIV3 = 4

These operators are applied in order of precedence:

Operator	Example
Brackets	( )
Signs	+, −
Multiplication and division	*, /, MOD, DIV
Addition and subtraction	+, −
Comparison	<,>,<=,!=
Boolean operators	AND, OR

Now test yourself

TESTED

1 Calculate the value assigned to the variable x if:
   (a) $x = (13-4)/3$
   (b) $x = 5*4/2$
   (c) $x = 13-2*4$
   (d) $x = 15MOD6$
   (e) $x = 29DIV2*3$

Programming constructs

REVISED

The program in the previous example was a simple sequential program.

Sequence

Execute the statements one after the other.

Selection

The path through the program is decided by looking at a condition.

Depending on the condition one of a set of alternative paths is followed.

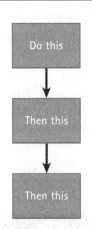

Figure 10.2 **A sequence**

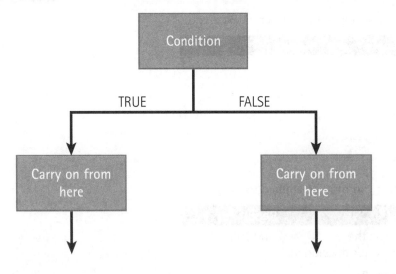

Sequence A program structure where a list of instructions is carried out one after the other.

Selection A program structure where the path taken is decided through the use of a condition (IF THEN).

Figure 10.3 **A decision based on a Boolean expression**

We can use the IF–THEN–ELSE structure to make decisions about which path to follow.

A simple thermostat program to control a heater:

```
if temp < 20 then
    turn on heater
else
    turn off heater
endif
```

We can add instructions to turn the heater off if the temperature reaches 22 degrees by extending this and nesting another IF command inside the first one.

```
if temp < 20 then
        turn on heater
else
        if temp >22 then
                turn off heater
        endif
endif
```
} One IF statement
   nested inside another

Iteration

To repeat a process based on a condition we use **iteration**.

We can use a count-controlled loop.

To print the 5 times table we could use the following program:

```
for k= 1 to 12
    print (k, "times 5 is ", k*5)
next k
```

We can also control the loop using a condition.

A WHILE loop repeats a section of code while a condition is true.

The same tables can be printed using a WHILE loop:

```
count=0
while count < 12:
    count= count +1
    print(count," times 5 is ",count*5)
endwhile
```

A REPEAT loop repeats a section of code until a condition is true.

The same tables can also be printed using a REPEAT loop:

```
count=0
repeat
    count= count +1
    print(count," times 5 is ",count*5)
until count==12
```

A WHILE loop checks the condition before the code section is executed.
● A WHILE loop may not be executed at all if the condition is met.

A REPEAT loop checks the condition after the code section has been executed.
● A REPEAT loop will always execute at least once.

> **Iteration** A program structure where a group of instructions is repeatedly executed while, or until, a condition is met (loop).

> **Exam tip**
>
> Questions including incorrectly formed loops are often set by examiners. Look for infinite loops where the condition is never going to be met or loops where the condition is not able to provide the expected output.

Comparison operators

In the examples on page 71, we have checked conditions by using:

```
while count<12
```

or

```
until count==12
```

The < and == are called comparison operators.

These comparisons will return TRUE or FALSE.

Comparison operator	Meaning	Examples
==	Is equal to	3 == 3 TRUE 3 == 5 FALSE
>	Is greater than	5>3 TRUE 5>9 FALSE
<	Is less than	3<5 TRUE 9<9 FALSE
!=	Is not equal to	3!=5 TRUE 5!=5 FALSE
<=	Is less than or equal to	3<=3 TRUE 9<=5 FALSE
>=	Is greater than or equal to	5>=3 TRUE 5>=9 FALSE

These operations can be combined using AND or OR to make more complex conditions.

AND

Requires both statements to be TRUE for the condition to return TRUE.

For example, checking for a fairground ride that someone is over 1.2 metres tall and aged 7 or over:

height> 1.2 AND age >=7

For this to be TRUE **both** conditions must be TRUE.

NOT

Reverses the output from a comparison.

We could also phrase this requirement so that it says the rider must be over 1.2 metres high and NOT less than 7 years of age.

height>1.2 AND NOT(age<7)

OR

Requires just one of the conditions to be TRUE for the condition to return TRUE.

Rephrasing the question by reversing the conditions means we could use OR and NOT to achieve the same result.

NOT(Height<1.2 OR age<7)

Requires **both** of these conditions to be FALSE for TRUE to be returned.

Condition	Explanation	Returns
(3>5) AND (5<6)	3>5 FALSE, 5<6 TRUE	FALSE
(3<=6) AND 7!=10	3<=6 TRUE, 7!=10 TRUE	TRUE
(3>5) OR (5<6)	3>5 FALSE, 5<6 TRUE	TRUE
NOT(3>5) AND (5<6)	NOT(3>5)TRUE, 5<6 TRUE	TRUE

> **Exam tip**
>
> You may be asked to identify an error in a code segment, check that the condition is correct and produces the desired output.

Now test yourself

TESTED ☐

2 What is returned by the following comparisons?
  (a) 3!=3
  (b) 3<5
  (c) 3<=3 AND 5>4
  (d) 8>=6 OR 5!=6
  (e) 3==5 OR 5<=5

String manipulation

REVISED ☐

String variables simply store a string of characters.

It is possible to manipulate the contents of a string using a range of functions.

Typically in a string, the characters are labelled from 0 upwards.

If text = "Computing"

0	1	2	3	4	5	6	7	8
C	o	m	p	u	t	i	n	g

Function	Explanation	Example
Length	Returns the length of the string.	text.length = 9
Substring	We can separate substrings by character position, or start and length.	text.substring(0) = "C" text.substring(3) = "p" text.substring(0:3) ="Com" text.substring(3:4) ="puti"
Concatenation	We can join two strings together by concatenating them usually with +.	If text1 ="ginger" and text2 ="cat" text1+text2 ="gingercat"
Case	We can use commands like upper and lower to change the case.	If text1 = "Bridge" text1.upper = "BRIDGE" text1.lower ="bridge"
ASCII conversion	To switch between the character and its ASCII code.	ASC(A) =65 CHR(65) ="A"

3 If text = "Revision" and name = "Frank" state the result returned by:
(a) text.length
(b) name + "'s " + text.lower
(c) name.upper
(d) text.substring(1:3)
(e) ASC(B)

Arrays

REVISED

When solving problems with a large number of variables all of the same description, rather than create these individually we assign the values to an array.

One-dimensional arrays

An array uses a single identifier (label) with an index value to create a set of variables.

For example, to store 10 names we can use the array names(10).

This creates 10 locations in memory labelled names(0), names(1) … names(9).

0	1	2	3	4	5	6	7	8	9
Henry	Alan	Jane	Li	Umar	Chen	Hannah	Abid	Mary	Keith

We can reference the contents using the index value. names(4) is Umar.

We can update the array by assigning a value to an element. The instruction names(2)= Ben will update the array to:

0	1	2	3	4	5	6	7	8	9
Henry	Alan	Ben	Li	Umar	Chen	Hannah	Abid	Mary	Keith

A one-dimensional array is like a list and we can use a simple 'for next' loop to access each of the elements in turn.

The program segment:

```
for i=0 to 9
   names(i) =input("Enter a name ")
next i
```

will allow the user to populate the array by typing in the names for each element.

Two-dimensional arrays

These can be used to store lists of lists, for example storing student names in their workgroups.

This array represents four groups of three students:

	0	1	2
0	Henry	Ben	Li
1	Umar	Chen	Hannah
2	Abid	Mary	Keith
3	Jenny	Imran	Jane

> **Exam tip**
>
> Note that computer scientists start counting at 0.

We reference the elements by row and column: names(2,1) is Mary.

To populate this array we could use a nested for next loop.

```
for i=0 to 3
  for j=0 to 2
    names(i,j) =input("Enter a name ")
  next j
next i
```

Exam tip

Note that arrays are usually defined by row then column when interpreted as a table, but check the question carefully in case the examiner chooses to use a different format.

TESTED

Now test yourself

4 For the array, fruit(r,c) if fruit(1,3) is Apple:

	0	1	2	3	4
0	Pear	Grape	Banana	Damson	Orange
1	Raspberry	Blueberry	Blackcurrant	Apple	Grapefruit
2	Strawberry	Greengage	Lemon	Lime	Kiwi

(a) What is the value of fruit(0,0)?
(b) What is the value of fruit(2,4)?
(c) What is the array element for 'Blueberry'?

Basic file-handling operations

REVISED

The array is a set of indexed variables stored in memory and, if the power is turned off, the data will be lost.

Files

To save data from a program it is necessary to write the data to a **file**.

The process for doing this is:
- open a file for write access
  - ○ (this will often create the file if it does not already exist)
- write the data from the program to the file
- close the file.

File Stored data saved on a suitable medium.

For example, to write the contents of a one-dimensional array to a text file called savednames:

```
open file for write access savednames.txt
for i = 0 to 9
  write names(i) to file
next i
close savednames.txt
```

To retrieve data stored in a file:
- open file for read access
- read the data from the file into the program
- close the file.

When reading data from a file we often do not know exactly how much data is stored. We can use an end-of-file marker to determine when all the data has been read:

```
Open file for read access
While NOT(EndOfFile)
    Read data from file into computer
Endwhile
Close file
```

To read in the data line by line and print it until it reaches the end of the data file:

```
open file for read access savednames.txt
j=0
while NOT end of file
    read from file to names(j)
    j=j+1
endwhile
close savednames.txt
```

> **Exam tip**
>
> Make sure you are familiar with the OCR pseudocode guide. Questions may be set using this. You do not have to use the OCR pseudocode in your answers, providing the logic is clear.

Records

Retrieving items from large amounts of data stored in a text file can be time consuming.

Databases use **records** to store data.

A record is structured by categories called fields or attributes.

> **Record** A data store organised by attributes (fields).

FIELDS

First_name	Last_name	Telephone	Email
Bill	Wilson	02223334441	bw@somemail.com
Graham	Mills	02224446667	graham@othermail.co.uk
Harry	Smith	01112224445	harry@othermail.co.uk
Sally	Jones	01113335557	sj@somemail.com

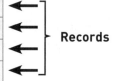 **Records**

Figure 10.4 Database table 'tblNames'

● A record requires all the fields to be set up before any data can be stored in it.
● The data in the fields must be the same type.
● There is a primary key that identifies each record in the database.

SQL

REVISED

Records can be manipulated using structured query language (SQL).
SELECT is used to select which fields from the table to return from the query.
FROM tells the query which table to select the data from.

```
SELECT "First_name", "E_mail" FROM "tblNames"
```

will return the data:

Bill, bw@somemail.com

Graham, graham@othermail.co.uk

Harry, harry@othermail.co.uk

Sally, sj@somemail.com

SELECT ★ tells the query to select all fields. The ★ is a wildcard meaning 'all values'.

WHERE tells the query there is a condition applied to which data to return.

```
SELECT * FROM "tblNames" WHERE "Last_name" = 'Jones'
```

Will return the data:

Sally, Jones, 01113335557, sj@somemail.com

LIKE allows us to use a wildcard % to replace any string of characters to identify multiple similar items.

```
SELECT "First_name", "Last_name" FROM "tblNames"
WHERE "E_mail" LIKE '%com'
```

Will select those records where the email includes any string followed by 'com' and will return:

Bill, Wilson

Sally, Jones

AND and **OR** can be used to combine conditions on the search criteria.

```
SELECT "First_name", "Last_name", "Telephone" FROM
"tblNames" WHERE "E_mail" LIKE '%com' AND "Last_
name" LIKE 'Wil%'
```

Will return:

Bill, Wilson, 02223334441

```
SELECT "Last_name", "E_Mail" FROM "tblNames" WHERE
"E_mail" LIKE '%com' OR "Telephone" LIKE '%6667'
```

Will return:

Wilson, bw@somemail.com

Mills, graham@othermail.co.uk

Jones, sj@somemail.com

For the data tblstock:

Item_No	Description	Stock	Price
121	Fork	56	1.10
131	Spoon	65	1.15
222	Plate	19	3.25
233	Bowl	17	4.25
245	Cup	34	3.95

5   What is returned by the following SQL statements?
   (a) SELECT "Item_No", "Description" FROM "tblstock" WHERE "Price" < '2.00'
   (b) SELECT * FROM "tblstock" WHERE "Stock" > '56'
   (c) SELECT "Description", "Stock" FROM "tblstock" WHERE "Item_No" LIKE '1%'
6   Write an SQL query to returns the Item_No and Description for all stock where the stock level is greater than 20 and the price is less than 3.00.

Functions and procedures

REVISED

Apart from simple linear programs, most programs will consist of several modules, each performing part of the task.

Functions and **procedures** are subprograms that are able to repeat a task within a program and so:
● reduce the overall size of the program
● make the code easier to understand and maintain by using named subprograms
● save time as they only need be written and tested once
● improve debugging because code need only be checked in one place
● minimise testing, saving time and minimising the chance of errors by reusing the many pre-written and tested procedures and functions.

> **Function** A subprogram that takes parameters and outputs a value.
>
> **Procedure** A subprogram to perform a specific task.

Functions

● Functions are called with some data (parameters).
● The data is processed by the function.
● The function returns a value to be used in place of the function.

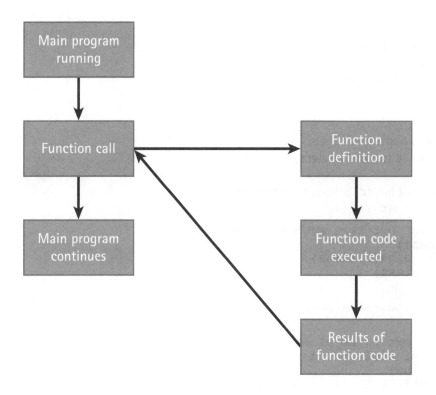

Figure 10.5 Calling a function

Functions are defined outside the main body of the program and require:
- a function name
- any parameters
- the code for the function
- the outputs (the value returned to the program).

Example

A simple function to calculate the area of a circle given the radius:
- function name 'area'
- parameters to be passed 'radius'
- the code area= 3.14159*radius*radius
- the output returned to the main program 'area'.

```python
# the function definition
def area(radius):
    area=3.14159*radius*radius
    return area

# the main body of the program
value=int(input("Enter the radius for the circle"))
print("Area of circle is")
print(area(value))
```

Figure 10.6 **The code for this in the Python programming language**

Procedures

The only major differences between a function and procedure are:

- procedures do not necessarily return a value
- procedures can act independently of the main program.

A procedure to print out some text a number of times:

- The procedure 'multiprint' is passed two parameters, 'text' and 'times'.
- It prints the text as many times as it is told to, then returns control to the main program, but no values are returned.

```
# the sub program to print out text several times
def multiprint(text,times):
                for i in range(0,times):
                    print(text)



# Main program
sampletext=input("input text to be printed")
value=int(input("number of times to be printed"))
multiprint(sampletext,value)
print("Now control is back with the main program")
```

Figure 10.7 **A procedure in the Python programming language to print text several times**

Exam practice

1 What is a variable?
2 How does a variable differ from a constant?
3 If the value input by the user is 2, what is the output from this program written in pseudocode?

```
i=0
input b
while i<b
    print i, i*i
    i=i+1
endwhile
```

4 Data is stored in a two-dimensional array name() with three rows and four columns. Write a pseudocode program to save this data to a file called names.txt.
5 The data table 'Cities' is shown below:

City	Country	Pop (100,000)	Currency
Birmingham	UK	1100	UKP
Birmingham	USA	212	USD
Detroit	USA	689	USD
Paris	France	2244	EURO
Barcelona	Spain	1602	EURO

State the output returned by the following SQL queries:

(a) SELECT "City", 'Pop' FROM "tblCities" WHERE "Currency" = 'UKP'

(b) SELECT "City", 'Country' FROM "tblCities" WHERE "Pop" > '1500'

Write a query to return:

(d) the city and population for all cities where the currency is the Euro.

(e) all the data about any city beginning with 'B' with a population less than 1000.

6 If text is "Functions and Procedures" calculate the value returned by:

(a) text.length

(b) text.substring(2,3)

(c) text.substring(13,5)

(d) State the command that returns the value "ions".

7 (a) What is the difference between a function and a procedure?

(b) Identify three advantages for a programmer in using functions and procedures to write a program.

ONLINE

Summary

You should now have an understanding of the following:

Variables and constants are labels for memory locations containing data to be used by a program.

- Variables can be changed by a program, constants cannot.
- Assignment is the allocation of a value to a variable or constant.

There are three main program structures:

- sequence: instructions carried out one after the other
- selection: a decision is used to determine which path to follow (IF THEN)
- iteration: a section of code is repeated (a loop).

Commands to manipulate strings include:

- length
- substrings
- concatenation
- change case
- ASCII/char conversion.

A one-dimenional array is a list of variables with the same name but a changing index value.

A two-dimensional array is a table of values with the same name indexed by row and column values.

Data can be saved from a program to a file using open for read/write, read/write, close.

Records are used by databases and the data is organised by attributes (fields).

- A record is a complete set of data for one item.

SQL is used to query records using:

- SELECT to select which fields to return
- FROM to identify the data table to use
- WHERE to set a condition on the data to return
- LIKE to identify the properties of a field for data to be returned
- wildcards to look for data similar to a condition.

Functions and procedures are subprograms that are defined outside the main body of the program and called by the program using parameters as necessary.

- A function usually returns a value; a procedure does not need to return a value.
- Both return control to the program once completed at the point where they were called.

11 Writing reliable programs

Defensive design

Thinking about potential problems before starting to code will eliminate many of them and improve the reliability of the system.

Input validation

A major source of problems is unexpected or erroneous input.

Validation can be used to check that any input values are possible and conform to a rule.

Data can be validated to make sure:
- it is the right type, e.g. integer, real, string or Boolean
- it is in the right range, e.g. between 1 and 10
- that required data is entered; a presence check
- it is in the right format, e.g. dates are in the form dd/mm/yyyy
- it is the right length, e.g. telephone numbers are 11 or 12 digits long.

Validation does not guarantee that the value is right; merely that it is possible and conforms to the rules for that input.

Input sanitisation

Input sanitisation checks and modifies any input before passing it on.

Sanitisation can use a whitelist or blacklist approach.

Whitelists:
- contain all the acceptable inputs to be accepted.
- take a long time to set up and are quite restrictive but are very secure.

Blacklists:
- contain all the unacceptable inputs to be rejected.
- may not include all unacceptable inputs making them less secure but less restrictive.

Input sanitisation sometimes includes features to modify input values to make them acceptable, for example replacing single quotes with double quotes or removing unwanted characters.

Planning ahead

There are situations that cannot be dealt with through input validation. Combinations of acceptable data may lead to unexpected outcomes, for example division by zero.
- When developing a program we know what data to input, the eventual end user may make different choices leading to unexpected problems.
- There may be users who deliberately try to break the program.

Anticipating such events and making the program deal with unexpected results will make the program more reliable. For example, exiting gracefully after an error, or trapping events, reporting them and restarting at a suitable point.

Planning for such contingencies is essential if we are to create a robust program. Programmers need to:

- use meaningful prompts for each input
- trap unexpected inputs
- anticipate misuse of the system and build in error-trapping for these events
- consider the combined effect of valid input values that are atypical and might lead to errors
- identify methods to authenticate the user for online systems.

Now test yourself

TESTED ☐

1 Identify two types of validation that can be applied to an input.
2 Why are whitelists preferable to blacklists for reliable input sanitisation?

Maintainability

REVISED ☐

Apart from the simplest programs, it is unlikely a program will be error-free in its first version.

Over time, the requirements for a program may change and the program will require some modification.

Programs need to be well structured and documented to ensure they are easily maintained.

- Logs showing the tests that have been carried out and the results will enable the maintenance programmer to eliminate these as sources of error and simplify the process of tracking down bugs.
- Indenting the program structures in the code will enable a maintenance programmer to follow the process more effectively, identifying loop entry and exit points.
- Adding comments to the code will identify what each section does and how the program is intended to work.
- Using meaningful variable names will help identify the purpose of each variable so that the maintenance programmer can see much more clearly what data should be expected at each point.

Testing

REVISED ☐

Iterative testing

Often called white box testing, this involves testing the program at every stage of the development process:

- Programs are checked at a modular level during development.
- As each new module is added, the program is tested to ensure that no errors have been introduced and data from previous modules works with the new module.
  - Faults that appear to be the result of one process may be a knock-on consequence of inputs from another module.
- Identifying faults in an individual module may be harder once they are combined.

Final/terminal testing

Often called black box testing, this involves testing that the final program functions as expected:
- Checking that the modules are correctly assembled into a working solution.
- Checking the program produces the desired results using real data and a typical end user.

Now test yourself

TESTED

3 What is meant by iterative testing?
4 Give one reason for final/terminal testing for a program.

Selecting and using suitable test data

To test a program effectively, it is necessary to identify suitable test data and the expected outcome.

Typically a test table will include:

Test	Data used	Reason for test	Expected outcome

Test data should contain the following types of data:

- **valid**: test data that is typical input for the system
- **valid extreme**: test data that is valid but at the extreme end of the range of acceptable input
- **invalid**: test data that is out of range and should be rejected
- **invalid extreme**: test data that is invalid but only just outside the limit for being acceptable
- **erroneous**: test data that should be rejected because it is the wrong type of input.

Syntax errors

Syntax errors occur when the language has not been used properly

Some examples of syntax errors include:
- variables not declared before use
- variables not declared properly before use
- incompatible variable types
- using assignments incorrectly, e.g. 3+4=x rather than x=3+4
- variable names incorrect, for example incorrect spelling or formatting.

Syntax error When the rules of the programming language are broken.

Logic errors

These are errors that occur at run time, for example errors generated because values in variables are not as expected.

Logic errors can generate a range of problems including:
- division by zero
- programs that do not complete
- the memory is filled with data and we get a stack overflow
- incorrect output
- the program will crash.

Logic error When the logical structure of the program produces an unexpected result.

The main causes of logic errors are:
- conditions that cannot be met in conditional statements
- divisors that can reach zero
- infinite loops
- incorrect algorithms (it doesn't do what it was meant to)
- incorrect expressions (calculations that are incorrect or missing brackets).

Now test yourself

TESTED

5 What is meant by a syntax error? Give an example of a syntax error.
6 What is meant by a logical error? Give an example of a logical error.

Exam practice

1 The following code will produce an error .

```
x = 100
y = 10
while y >0
    y = y - 1
    t = x/y
    print t
endwhile
```

(a) What is the error?
(b) What kind of error is this?
(c) Rewrite the code to fix the error.
2 A program to calculate a price including VAT at 20% requires the user to input a non-VAT price. Draw a test table including four different tests that could be applied to the input.
3 Describe what is meant by a whitelist and a blacklist in input sanitisation.
4 Describe three features that will make code more maintainable.

ONLINE

Summary

You should now have an understanding of the following:
Input validation can check that data conforms to a rule.
- Input validation checks that data is permitted, not that it is correct.

Input sanitisation uses a whitelist to identify permitted inputs and a blacklist to identify unacceptable inputs.
- Input sanitisation can also modify some inputs to make them acceptable.

Programs can be more robust if they are planned carefully and suitable error-trapping is built in.

Features to make code easier to maintain include:
- indents
- meaningful variable names

- test results
- annotation.

Iterative testing is carried out on each module as it is developed.

Final testing is carried out once the modules are combined into a final product to check that they work in combination with each other.

Testing should include valid, invalid, extreme and erroneous data.

Syntax errors are the result of the program rules being broken.

Logic errors occur at run time when the logical structure of the program produces an unexpected result.

12 Computational logic

We use binary to store data in a computer because of the ease with which we can represent two states using a simple electronic circuit.

The memory in a computer uses circuits made from transistors and capacitors to hold a single value, 0 or 1.

By wiring these transistors and capacitors together in various ways we can create circuits that can make simple logical calculations.

These simple circuits are called **logic gates**.

> **Logic gate** A circuit that produces an output based on the inputs.

NOT gate REVISED ☐

NOT gate: symbol ¬

> **NOT** Reverses the input.

The NOT gate reverses the input.

A	P
0	1
1	0

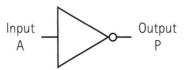

Figure 12.1 NOT gate

AND gate REVISED ☐

AND gate: symbol ∧

The AND gate outputs 1 only if both inputs are 1, otherwise it outputs 0.

> **AND** Outputs 1 if both inputs are 1.

A	B	P
0	0	0
0	1	0
1	0	0
1	1	1

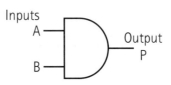

Figure 12.2 AND gate

OR gate REVISED ☐

OR gate: symbol ∨

The OR gate outputs 1 if either or both of the inputs is 1, 0 if both inputs are 0.

> **OR** Outputs 1 if one, or both, of the inputs is 1.

A	B	P
0	0	0
0	1	1
1	0	1
1	1	1

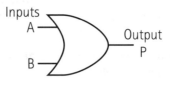

Figure 12.3 OR gate

Complete the diagrams by inserting the missing data.

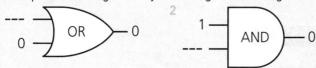

Combining logic gates

REVISED

We can combine these logic gates to create more complex **logic circuits**.

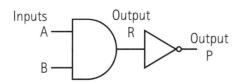

> **Logic circuit** A circuit made up by combining logic gates.

Figure 12.4 AND and NOT gates forming a NAND gate

The logic for this circuit can be worked out by using a **truth table**.

> **Truth table** A method for recording all the possible input and output combinations for a logic circuit.

A	B	R = A AND B	P = NOT R
0	0	0	1
0	1	0	1
1	0	0	1
1	1	1	0

More complex circuits with three inputs require larger truth tables showing all the possible combinations.

The circuit for (A AND B) OR C:

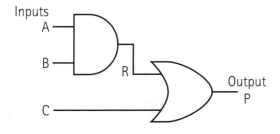

Figure 12.5 More complex logic circuit

There are three inputs so we need to consider eight possible combinations.

A	B	C	R = A AND B	P = R OR C
0	0	0	0	0
0	0	1	0	1
0	1	0	0	0
0	1	1	0	1
1	0	0	0	0
1	0	1	0	1
1	1	0	1	1
1	1	1	1	1

Complete the truth tables.

3 P = A AND (B AND C)

A	B	C	B AND C	P = A AND (B AND C)
0	0	0	0	0
0	0	1	0	
0	1	0	0	
0	1	1	1	
1	0	0		
1	0	1		
1	1	0		
1	1	1		

4 P = A OR (NOT B AND C)

A	B	C	NOT B AND C	P = A OR (NOT B AND C)
0	0	0	0	0
0	0	1	1	
0	1	0		
0	1	1		
1	0	0	0	
1	0	1		
1	1	0	0	
1	1	1		

Boolean algebra

REVISED

We use a form of algebra to write down these circuits.

The one above would be written as: $P = (A \land B) \lor C$.

Another example of a Boolean expression is $P = (A \lor B) \land C$.

The diagram for this is:

> **Boolean algebra** A method for expressing logic circuits mathematically.

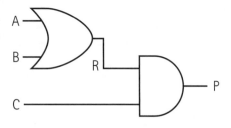

Figure 12.6 Combined logic gates

And the truth table is:

A	B	C	R = A ∨ B	P = R ∧ C
0	0	0	0	0
0	0	1	0	0
0	1	0	1	0
0	1	1	1	1
1	0	0	1	0
1	0	1	1	1
1	1	0	1	0
1	1	1	1	1

Exam practice

1 What is the output from this circuit?

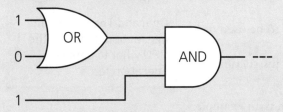

2 Complete this truth table for P=A AND NOT B.

A	B	P= A AND NOT B
0	0	0
0	1	
1	0	
1	1	

3 Draw truth tables for the expressions:
   (a) NOT(A OR B)
   (b) A OR NOT(B AND C)

ONLINE

Summary

You should now have an understanding of the following:
- Computers use binary because it is easy to tell the state of a switch, high/low, True/False, 0/1.
- The fundamental logic gates are AND, OR and NOT.

- These gates can be combined to form logic circuits.
- Truth tables are used to show all the possible input combinations and the resulting outputs.
- Boolean algebra is a way of expressing logic circuits mathematically.

13 Translators and language facilities

Translators

REVISED

Computers work in binary and the processor runs programs that are binary patterns.

These instructions consist of two parts:
- the operation to be carried out, the **opcode**
- the data to be used with the operation, **operand**.

10110000	01100001
opcode	operand

The operand is most often an address, either to locate data to be used or to send data to.
- Some opcodes do not have an operand, for example the instruction telling the program to stop.

Instructions in pure binary are called machine code, which is an example of a low-level language that works deep down on the hardware and not high up at the user interface level.

Programs are generally written using a high-level language that the computer cannot use directly.

Translators are used to convert the high-level programming language to low-level machine code for the computer to process.

> **Translator** A program that converts high-level or assembly-level commands into machine commands.
>
> **Opcode** The part of an instruction that tells the CPU what operation is to be done.
>
> **Operand** The part of an instruction that tells the CPU what to apply the operation to.

Assemblers

REVISED

Assembly language is a low-level language that uses a mnemonic to represent the binary opcode.

The opcode in the example above means 'move a value from a location to the Accumulator'.

If the binary is replaced by a suitable mnemonic such as MOV AL, it becomes easier for the programmer to work with.

If we also convert the operand to hexadecimal the instruction becomes much more memorable for the programmer

```
MOV AL 61
```

This assembly language command cannot be used directly by the processor, but each command represents a single command in machine code.

A translator called an assembler will translate these mnemonics into the pure binary required by the processor.

> **Assembler** Software that translates assembly language programs into machine code.

> **Exam tip**
>
> Making binary instructions easier to remember is one of the reasons for using hexadecimal in computers.

Compilers and interpreters

High-level languages are more like human languages and make writing programs easier.

Each high-level instruction will generally represent several machine code instructions.

The high-level language program needs to be translated into suitable machine code to be executed.

An interpreter translates each line of high-level code into the equivalent machine code then executes it before translating the next line.

A compiler will translate the complete program from **source code** (the original high-level program) into **object code** (the low-level machine code program that can be executed by the processor)

> **Source code** The program written by the programmer in a high-level language before it is converted into machine code.
>
> **Object code** The machine code produced by the translator to be run on the computer.

Table 13.1 **Advantages and disadvantages of interpreters**

Advantages	Disadvantages
Since it translates a line at a time it is easier to debug the code.	The code runs more slowly than compiled code because it needs to be translated each time it is run.
Errors are reported line by line as they are processed.	The source code is made available to the user meaning the user can modify the code.
Useful for experimenting with code with no need to recompile every time.	The user requires a copy of the translator in memory occupying space in memory.
The program can be run on any machine for which there is a suitable interpreter.	The code does not get optimised.

Table 13.2 **Advantages and disadvantages of compilers**

Advantages	Disadvantages
The executable file is unreadable meaning the user cannot modify the program (securing some of the programmer's intellectual property).	When developing code it needs to be recompiled after every change to the code.
Compiled code runs faster.	Errors are produced as a long list after compilation. It is difficult to try out ideas given the code needs to be recompiled and error lists examined after each modification.
There is no need for a translator to be in memory to run the code saving space and possibly cost.	Compiled code is specific to a processor and will not work on another type.
Compilers optimise the code to make it more efficient and effective.	

Now test yourself

1 What is source code?
2 What is object code?
3 Why do programs need to be translated before being run on a computer?

Integrated Development Environment (IDE)

An IDE is a software tool providing many of the utilities required to develop a program.

Editor

An editor for the source code to include features to:

- identify command words
- identify and indent loops
- identify variables
- indicate potential errors through colour coding.

```
num=int(input('Enter a number '))
for i in range(num,0,-2):
    print(i)
```

Figure 13.1 A program written using a specialised programming editor with pretty printing

Error diagnostics

- Tools for debugging code such as the ability to inspect variables.
- Step-by-step progression through a program.

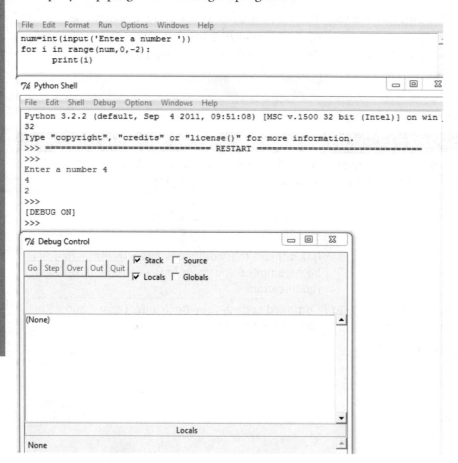

Figure 13.2 A debugger in use

Run-time environments

The necessary features to run a program:
- often for a different platform using a **virtual machine**
- no tools to change the program.

A build feature

- To compile and link other elements into the program.
- A translator, a compiler and possibly an interpreter.

> **Virtual machine** An emulation of a particular computer system or platform that allows programs intended to run on one computer system to run on a different one.

Now test yourself

TESTED

4 List three components of a typical IDE.
5 What is a virtual machine?

Exam practice

1 Identify three differences between an interpreter and a compiler.
2 Explain one difference between a high-level language and a low-level language.
3 What are the advantages of compiling a program for commercial distribution?
4 A developer may use an interpreter while developing a program then compile it for distribution. What are the advantages of using an interpreter at the development stage?

ONLINE

Summary

You should now have an understanding of the following:

Computers run programs given to them as a set of instructions; these instructions must be in binary. These binary-coded instructions are called machine code.

Assembly languages use mnemonics to represent the binary machine code instructions to make the code more readable for a human.

Each assembly language instruction is equivalent to a single machine code instruction.

High-level languages are similar to human language and are translated into machine code by a translator.

Each high-level command is equivalent to several machine instructions.

Compilers are translators that translate the whole of the source code into object code before running the program.

Interpreters convert the source code one line at a time, running the code before moving on to the next line.

An IDE is an Integrated Development Environment that provides utilities to develop a program, often made up of:
- an editor: software used for writing the source code
- error diagnostics: used to debug programs during development
- a run-time environment: a facility to run the program

14 Data representation

Units

Computers work in **binary**; the basic unit is the binary digit or bit, 1 or 0.

8 bits (b)	1 byte (B)
1000 B	1 kilobyte (kB)
1000 kB	1 megabyte (MB)
1000 MB	1 gigabyte (GB)
1000 GB	1 terabyte (TB)
1000 TB	1 petabytes (PB)

Numbers

The computer works in binary so all data needs to be represented in binary.

Converting binary to denary

To convert a binary number to **denary** (base 10 or decimal) add the column values where there is a 1 in the binary number.

> **Example**
>
> Convert the binary number 10001011 to denary.
>
> | 128 | 64 | 32 | 16 | 8 | 4 | 2 | 1 |
> |---|---|---|---|---|---|---|---|
> | 1 | 0 | 0 | 0 | 1 | 0 | 1 | 1 |
> | 128 | | | | +8 | | +2 | +1 |
>
> =139 in denary.

Binary A number system based on 2, using just two symbols: 1 and 0.

Denary A number system based on 10 using the digits 0–9.

Converting denary to binary

Divide repeatedly by 2, recording the remainder until the answer is 0.

> **Example**
>
> Convert the denary number 155 to binary.
>
> | 155 | ÷ | 2 | = | 77 | REM | 1 | This is the number of 1s |
> |---|---|---|---|---|---|---|---|
> | 77 | ÷ | 2 | = | 38 | REM | 1 | This is the number of 2s |
> | 38 | ÷ | 2 | = | 19 | REM | 0 | This is the number of 4s |
> | 19 | ÷ | 2 | = | 9 | REM | 1 | This is the number of 8s |
> | 9 | ÷ | 2 | = | 4 | REM | 1 | This is the number of 16s |
> | 4 | ÷ | 2 | = | 2 | REM | 0 | This is the number of 32s |
> | 2 | ÷ | 2 | = | 1 | REM | 0 | This is the number of 64s |
> | 1 | ÷ | 2 | = | 0 | REM | 1 | This is the number of 128s |
>
> OR
>
> | 128 | 64 | 32 | 16 | 8 | 4 | 2 | 1 |
> |---|---|---|---|---|---|---|---|
> | 1 | 0 | 0 | 1 | 1 | 0 | 1 | 1 |
>
> 155 in denary is 10011011 in binary.

Now test yourself

TESTED ☐

1 Convert the following to denary.
   (a) 00001101
   (b) 10100001
   (c) 11001100
2 Convert the following to binary.
   (a) 35
   (b) 167
   (c) 200

Binary addition

REVISED ☐

When adding two binary numbers we only have four possibilities:

0+0 =0, 1+0 = 1, 0+1=1 and 1+1 = 10 (2 in denary).

In the case of 1+1 we need to write down the 0 and carry the 1 to the next column.

This gives us a fifth possibility 1+1+1= 11 (3 in denary).

In this case, we write down the 1 and carry a 1 to the next column.

Example

```
      0  0  0  1  0  1  1  1
+     1  0  0  0  1  1  1  0
                        0  1
Carry                1
```
In this case 1 + 1 = 10 so we write down the 0 and carry the 1 to the next column

```
      0  0  0  1  0  1  1  1
+     1  0  0  0  1  1  1  0
                  1  0  1
Carry          1  1
```
In this case 1 + 1 + 1= 11 so we write down the 1 and carry the 1 to the next column

Completing the process

```
      0  0  0  1  0  1  1  1
+     1  0  0  0  1  1  1  0
      1  0  1  0  0  1  1  1
Carry       1  1  1  1
```

Now test yourself

TESTED ☐

3 Add the following in binary:
   (a) 01010111 + 00001001
   (b) 10001100 + 00111111

Overflow

Example

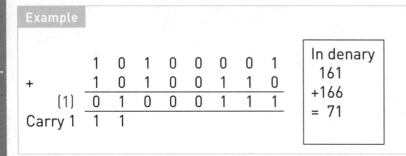

```
        1 0 1 0 0 0 0 1      In denary
    +   1 0 1 0 0 1 1 0         161
    (1) 0 1 0 0 0 1 1 1       +166
Carry 1 1 1                   = 71
```

Exam tip

Show your working in binary for these and make sure you include carries. If the working is shown you may gain some credit even with a minor error. It is acceptable to check your answer by converting to denary, but only as a check.

The two 1s in the left-most column in the example above have generated a carry for a ninth column.

● The result of the calculation is too big to fit into 8 bits.
● This is called overflow and the result will be incorrect.

Overflow can generate logical errors, i.e. the results are not as expected and the program may crash because it cannot deal with the overflow digit.

Binary shifts

Moving the binary digits left or right is known as a binary shift (or logical shift).

Moving to the left multiplies the value by two for each place the value is shifted.

Moving to the right divides the value by two for each place the value is shifted.

Example

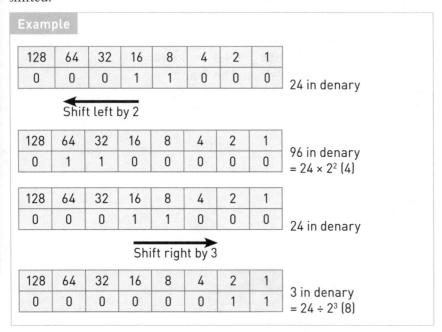

128	64	32	16	8	4	2	1
0	0	0	1	1	0	0	0

24 in denary

← Shift left by 2

128	64	32	16	8	4	2	1
0	1	1	0	0	0	0	0

96 in denary = 24×2^2 (4)

128	64	32	16	8	4	2	1
0	0	0	1	1	0	0	0

24 in denary

Shift right by 3 →

128	64	32	16	8	4	2	1
0	0	0	0	0	0	1	1

3 in denary = $24 \div 2^3$ (8)

Of course if we shift the value by too much we risk losing 1s at either end resulting in overflow or (underflow), losing the accuracy of the value stored.

Now test yourself

4 Complete the following multiplications and divisions for the binary values.
   (a) 00011100 multiplied by 8   (b) 11001100 divided by 4

Hexadecimal (Hex)

Hexadecimal numbers are base 16 values.

- We need 16 symbols to represent the digits.
- To represent the digits 10 to 15 we use the symbols A to F.

The table shows the values of each hex digit in denary and binary.

> **Hexadecimal (hex)** A number system based on 16 using the digits 0–9 and A–F to represent the denary values 0–15.

Denary	Hex	Binary	Denary	Hex	Binary
0	0	0000	8	8	1000
1	1	0001	9	9	1001
2	2	0010	10	A	1010
3	3	0011	11	B	1011
4	4	0100	12	C	1100
5	5	0101	13	D	1101
6	6	0110	14	E	1110
7	7	0111	15	F	1111

Converting hex to denary

The column values for hex numbers are 1s, 16s etc.

> **Example**
>
> 5A from hex to denary:
>
> | 16 | 1 |
> |----|---|
> | 5 | A |
>
> The denary equivalent of A is 10 so this = 5×16 + 10×1 = 90.

Converting denary to hex

Divide by 16 repeatedly then record the remainders:

> **Example**
>
> 171 from denary to hex:
>
> | 171 | ÷ | 16 | = | 10 | REM | 11 | This is the number of 1s (B) |
> |-----|---|----|---|----|-----|----|------------------------------|
> | 11 | ÷ | 16 | = | 0 | REM | 10 | This is the number of 16s (A) |
>
> 171 in denary is AB in hex.

Converting hex to binary

Converting from hex to binary is simply a case of replacing the hex with the equivalent binary nibble (4 bits).

> **Example**
>
> 3D in hex to binary:
>
> | 3 | D |
> |------|------|
> | 0011 | 1101 |
>
> 3D in hex is 00111101 in binary.

Converting binary to hex

Split the binary into nibbles and replace each nibble with its hex equivalent.

Example

10110010 in binary to hex:

1011	0010
B	2

10110010 in binary is B2 in hex.

This simple conversion between binary and hex is why we see hex used so frequently in computer science. Hex is much easier to remember than binary and reduces the chances of errors compared to typing in binary values.

Now test yourself   TESTED ☐

5 Convert the following binary numbers to hexadecimal.
   (a) 00111011   (b) 11000111   (c) 11111011
6 Convert the following hexadecimal numbers to binary.
   (a) 49   (b) 5C   (c) AD
7 Convert the following hexadecimal numbers to denary.
   (a) 5C   (b) A6   (c) AF
8 Convert the following denary numbers to hexadecimal.
   (a) 85   (b) 164   (c) 175

Check digits   REVISED ☐

When data is transferred, it is possible for this data to be corrupted.

Data typed in by a user, for example a credit card number, can be mistyped.

To minimise the errors associated with this, we use check digits.

Check digits are additional digits calculated from the number and appended to the number.

When data is received or input, the calculation is repeated to see if the check digit is the same. If not, an error is reported and the data requested again.

One simple check digit is the parity check for binary numbers.

For even parity, an additional digit is used to make sure the number of 1s is an even number.

For odd parity this would be an odd number of 1s.

Example

To transfer the seven-digit binary value 1101000 using even parity.

There are three 1s so we append an additional 1 to make this an even number and transmit 11010001.

If the fifth bit was corrupted we would transmit 11011001 which has five 1s and would be rejected and a request to resend the data issued.

TESTED

Now test yourself

9 A computer is using parity checking. One of the following items has been corrupted during transmission. Which one and how can you tell?

10011001, 11111111, 11110001, 10101010.

Other examples of numbers using check digits are:
- ISBN (book numbers)
- product codes (bar codes)
- credit card numbers.

Characters

REVISED

When you press the key on a computer keyboard a code is generated that the computer can convert into a symbol for display or printing.

These codes, as with all data on a computer, are binary.

It is clearly important all computer systems agree on these codes and their meanings if the data is to make any sense.

Character set

The **character set** of a computer is a list of all the characters available to the computer and the agreed associated codes.

> **Character set** The complete set of characters available to a computer.

ASCII

ASCII originally used a 7-bit code to represent the alphanumeric characters and a range of symbols and special characters.

This system could represent 2^7 or 128 characters.

The ASCII set was extended to 8 bits making it possible to represent a much larger character set, 2^8 or 256 characters.

> **ASCII** A 7-bit code to represent a set of characters available to a computer.

Unicode

Unicode originally used 16 bits to represent the character set making it possible to represent 2^{16} or over 65,000 characters, enough to include many foreign language symbols and a wide range of specialist symbols in the character set.

Unicode has been extended further using a series of code pages to represent the chosen language symbols. Unicode is capable of representing billions of characters.

Unicode has replaced the ASCII system but still allocates the same numeric values to the original ASCII symbols.

ASCII can be considered as a subset of Unicode.

> **Unicode** A character set that uses code pages to provide a range of language symbols. There are several billion possible character codes available to Unicode.

Images

Images are stored as a series of **pixels**, or dots, in binary.

In this simple two-colour example, the image can be stored in just 8 bytes:

> **Pixel** The smallest element of an image. These are the dots that make up the image on screen.

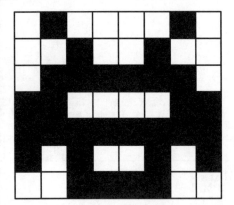

Figure 14.1 Space invader image in 8 bytes

To store just two colours we need 1 bit per pixel.

To store more than two colours we will need more bits per pixel:
- 2 bits to store 4 (2^2) colours per pixel.
- 3 bits to store 8 (2^3) colours per pixel.

Basically n bits will store 2^n colours per pixel.

For example with 16 bits, we can store 2^{16} or 65,536 colours.

- The number of bits used is called the **colour depth** (or bit depth).
- The greater the colour depth the more colours we can represent, but the more space we need to store the image.
- The **resolution** of the image is the number of pixels per unit (e.g. pixels per inch) or dpi (dots per inch).
- The higher the resolution the larger the file required to store the data.

> **Colour depth (bit depth)** The number of bits used to represent each pixel.
>
> **Resolution** The number of pixels (or dots) per unit, e.g. dots per inch (dpi), or pixels per inch, ppi.

Since the data stored is simply a set of binary numbers, the computer needs to be told various things including:
- the size in terms of height and width
- the colour depth.

These and other information are stored with the image.

Figure 14.2 The same image with eight colours and with just four colours

This data about the data is called **metadata**.

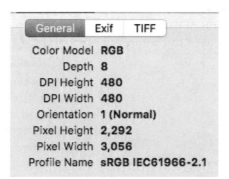

Figure 14.3 Some of the metadata stored with an image

14 Data representation

> **Metadata** Information stored with a file to enable the computer to interpret the data, for example to recreate the image from the binary data.

Sound

REVISED

Sound is a continuously varying (**analogue**) value.

In order to store this as a series of binary values, the sound is sampled at intervals and these values recorded.

The frequency of the intervals is the **sample rate** (or sampling frequency).
- The sample rate is expressed in kHz (thousands of samples per second).

> **Analogue** Continuously varying data.
>
> **Sample rate (Sampling frequency)** The number of times a sound is sampled per second measured in kHz.

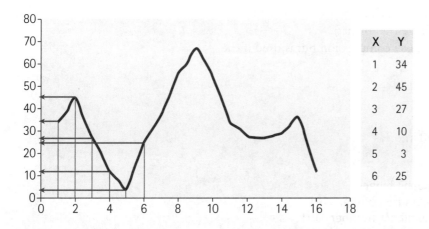

X	Y
1	34
2	45
3	27
4	10
5	3
6	25

Figure 14.4 Sound is sampled at set intervals

> **Exam tip**
>
> Do not confuse sample rate and bit rate: the sample rate is how frequently the sample is taken; the bit rate how much data is kept for each sample point. Sample rate is sometimes called sampling frequency.

- The more frequently the sound is sampled (the higher the sample rate), the closer to the original it will be.
- A typical CD quality sound is sampled at 44kHz.

Another factor affecting the quality of the sound is the accuracy of the data stored at each point.
- Using more bits to store each sample (the **bit depth**) will improve the quality of the sound recorded.

The **bit rate** is the number of samples stored per second of sampled sound and bit rate = sample rate × bit depth.
- The higher the sample rate and bit depth, the closer to the original sound it is but more data is stored and a larger file is needed to store the data.

> **Bit depth** The number of bits used to store each sound sample.
>
> **Bit rate** The number of bits used to store a second of sampled sound.

Compression

In order to display items in browsers, to store large items of data on portable media or to transfer it across the internet, we need to compress the data to make it smaller.

There are two types of **compression**.

> **Compression** Reducing the file size to reduce download times and storage requirements.

Lossy

Some of the data is removed:
- algorithms remove some of the data least likely to be noticed
- the original file cannot be restored from the data
- file formats include MP3 and JPEG which are popular formats for sound and images
- MP3 and JPEG allow for music and images to be downloaded quickly and the loss in quality is rarely noticeable.

Lossless

None of the data is removed but it is reorganised so that the original file can be reconstructed from the information stored:
- algorithms look for patterns in the data so that repeated data items can be stored just once along with the information to restore the data back into the original location
- the original data file can be recovered
- file formats using lossless compression include FLAC (Free lossless audio code) and TIFF (Tagged image file format)
- the size is not reduced as much as lossy compression but is used if the original must be restored.

Exam practice

1 Convert the decimal number 193 into:
   (a) binary
   (b) hexadecimal
2 Complete the binary shift using 8-bit binary:
   (a) two places to the left on the binary number 1101
   (b) two places to the right on the binary number 1101
   (c) convert the values of the results to denary
   (d) explain what has happened.
3 (a) Add the 8-bit binary numbers 10001110 and 11000000. Show your working.
   (b) Convert these binary values and the result to denary.
   (c) Explain what has happened.
4 What is meant by the character set of a computer?
5 How do the bit depth and sample rate affect a sampled digital sound and the file used to store it.
6 What is the bit depth for an image?
7 Identify two advantages for lossy compression over lossless compression for a music file.

Summary

You should now have an understanding of the following:

- All data in a computer is stored in binary.

- The computer uses electronic circuits to store binary using a switch with two possible states.

- Hexadecimal is often used by programmers because it is easy to convert to and from binary and is much easier to write, remember and identify than binary.

- Check digits are calculated values added to data that is transmitted that can be recalculated and checked by the receiver to identify any errors in transmission.

- The character set of a computer is all the characters that are available to it.

- ASCII is a 7-bit code representing the standard alphanumeric characters and important symbols.

- Unicode uses code pages to represent potentially billions of possible characters.

- The same numeric values are used within Unicode for the set of ASCII characters.

- Images are stored in binary using pixels.

- Pixels are the smallest element in an image.

- The number of bits per pixel determines how many colours each pixel can represent. This is called the colour or bit depth.

- The resolution of an image is the height and width of the image, usually in pixels per inch.

- The higher the resolution and the bit depth, the better the quality of the image and the larger the file required to store the image.

- Metadata stored with the image tells the computer how to interpret the data to reproduce the original image.

- Sound is sampled to convert it from an analogue quantity to a digital one.

- The quality of the sound sampled depends upon the number of bits per sample, the bit depth.

- The sample rate and bit depth determine the quality of the sound.

- The larger the bit depth and sample rate, the larger the file required to store the data.

- Compression is used to reduce the file size for storage or transmission.

- Lossy compression will reduce the file size most but some data will be lost and the quality reduced.

- Lossless compression does not lose any data but is not able to reduce the file size by as much as lossy compression.

Now test yourself answers

Chapter 1

1 The CPU is responsible for completing all the processing in the computer by following a set of instructions.

2 The number of instructions per second that the CPU can carry out, usually measured in GHz.

3 The data and instructions are both stored in binary in the same memory.

4 (a) MAR stores data being transferred between the CPU and memory.

   (b) ACC stores the results of any calculation in the ALU.

   (c) ALU completes arithmetic or logical calculations.

5 The PC is incremented at the end of the fetch phase (updated if the instruction requires a jump to a new location in the program).

6 The control unit decodes the instruction (also sends signals to control how data is moved about the CPU and memory).

7 Cache memory is fast memory close to or part of the CPU that stores data waiting to be processed/ frequently used data.

8 Each core can process instructions so a multi-core processor can process multiple instructions simultaneously improving the computer performance.

Chapter 2

1 RAM is volatile and data is lost when power is turned off/ ROM is non-volatile and does not lose its content when the power is turned off.

2 RAM holds the operating system and any applications and data currently in use.

3 ROM holds the data and instructions required to start the computer when the power is turned on (the boot process/ boot sequence).

Chapter 3

1 Operating system, applications and the user's data.

2 SSD are more robust, and have faster access times than magnetic hard disks.

3 Blu-ray Disc.

4 Three from capacity, (transfer/access) speed, portability, durability (robustness), reliability and cost.

5 200 × 6 MB = 1.2 GB which can be stored on a DVD or a USB flash drive.

(It does not specify postal system so cloud options are also possible.)

Chapter 4

1 LAN small geographical area, WAN large geographical area. WAN uses telecoms connection, LAN does not require them to connect the LAN.

2 Any two of:
   - Files are stored centrally so easily located and tracked.
   - System can be backed up centrally.
   - Software can be installed and updated centrally.
   - Good security features, e.g. personal login and password, different access levels for user groups, centralised anti-malware software.
   - Centralised file server means fewer duplicated files and applications.

3 Any two of:
   - Easy to set up, simply connect to other devices on the network directly.
   - Limited costs involved with no file server required.
   - Does not depend upon the server so continues to work when another device fails.

4 Fibre not subject to interference or signal degradation over long distances.

5 Faster and more secure (not easy to intercept the signal on a cable).

6 DNS converts easily understood URL into an IP address for the server holding the information required.

7 Any advantage from:
   - No need to update software accessed from these remote providers.
   - Access to data and applications from any internet connected computer.
   - No need to worry about data being backed up.
   - Easy to share files with colleagues worldwide.
   - No need to maintain your own network to store data.
   - No need for expensive support staff

Any disadvantage from:
   - You are entrusting your data to someone outside your organisation.

- Some of these servers and data centres are in countries with different legislation meaning sensitive data might not be secure.
- You trust that the service will be there when you need it, i.e. they are still in business.
- The provider continues to support the software you require.

Chapter 5

1 Fewer connections required.

2 Radio signals radiate in all directions and the signal can be intercepted by any enabled device.

3 A MAC address is a unique value set at the manufacturing stage; an IP address is allocated to a device on a network.

4 Any four of:
- sender's IP address
- receiver's IP address
- protocol
- packet number
- length of packet
- data
- end of packet marker
- error correction data.

5 Data is divided up into packets and encapsulated.

Individual data packets are sent via any available route to the destination.

Using the data added when encapsulated the original data can be error-checked and reassembled into the correct order.

6 The application layer supplies the data in a form that the receiving application can make use of.

Chapter 6

1 A computer program, often hidden inside another program, that reproduces itself and usually causes damage such as deleting files.

2 Software that interferes with the operation of the user's computer, for example encrypting the storage, or threatens to unless a sum of money is paid.

3 Any three from:
- Use up to date anti-malware software.
- Updates the operating system regularly to fix vulnerabilities.
- Don't open email attachments unless you are certain they are safe.
- Turn off images in email; malware can be embedded within the image.
- Don't open email from unknown senders.
- Avoid peer-to-peer sharing unless files can be scanned on download.
- Update web browsers to fix vulnerabilities.

4 An attempt to make a system unusable by flooding it with requests.

5 An attempt to obtain sensitive personal data.
- An email is sent supposedly from a trusted source, e.g. a bank, ebay, paypal.
- The email refers to a problem with your account and you to click on a link.
- The link then asks for account details.

6 Any two from:
- Don't open any links within these emails.
- Delete the email.
- Contact the supposed sender directly to confirm if it is genuine or not.

7 Firewalls are either software or hardware or both, placed between the network (or node) and other networks (or nodes) to control what comes in and what goes out.

8 It uses an encryption key to scramble the data and a decryption key to unscramble it. If the data is stolen or intercepted the thief cannot read the data with the decryption key.

Chapter 7

1 Network technicians will prefer to communicate with the operating system using a command line interface because they can issue single powerful commands to efficiently manage the system.

2 Icons represent actions or applications so easily recognised features, e.g. printer icons similar in all applications, no need to type commands simply select the appropriate icon.

3 Many calls require standard information and provide standard evidence. A voice recognition system is able to handle these meaning fewer human call handlers required.

4 Any two from:
- Managing the computer hardware and peripherals.
- Managing programs installed and being run.
- Managing data transfer between memory locations, the CPU and secondary storage.
- Providing the interface between the hardware and the applications.
- Providing an interface between the computer and user and managing the video display on screen.
- Managing security and organising data so that it is not overwritten.
- Providing a file system for the storage and retrieval of files.

5 Different users use different applications.

To keep files for each user secure.

Access levels, one may be admin others simply users unable to modify settings, add programs etc.

6 Any two from:
   – System clean up that will identify temporary files, cached copies of files and unused files that can be removed safely leaving more free space on the hard disk.
   – Anti-virus/malware to identify and remove malware from a system.
   – Encryption software to secure data using a suitable key to make it secure from any unauthorised user who access it.
   – Compression software to compress files into a smaller file for transfer to a smaller device or for electronic transmission.
   – Backup to make copies of files in case of loss or damage.
   – Other possibilities might include:
     – disk free space calculator
     – calendar
     – clock settings
     – file search facilities.

Chapter 8

1 National security, crime and taxation, data kept for domestic purposes.
2 Freedom of Information Act (2000)
3 Computer Misuse Act (1990)
4 Monitor posts detrimental to the organisation on social media.

   Monitor access to unacceptable websites while at work to avoid damage to the organisation/ monitor illegal activity.

   Monitor if the employee is working or simply browsing/booking holidays etc. to ensure employee is not using organisations facilities for non work-related activities.
5 Airplanes move very quickly in a three-dimensional space. Impossible for a pilot to see all of the airplanes in the space near to the aircraft. Not possible to react quickly enough once seen or detected. Consistent reaction with systems working cooperatively to avoid a collision, not possible to do this by pilot-to-pilot communication.

Chapter 9

1 Abstraction.
2 Breaking a problem down in sub-problems.
3 Linear because the list is unordered.
4 The merge sort would create several thousand separate lists and take up a lot of memory.
5 Insertion sort is good for checking that data is in order.
6 The merge sort uses a lot of memory but is efficient for large sets of data compared to the bubble or insertion sort techniques.

Chapter 10

1 (a) 3   (b) 10   (c) 5   (d) 3   (e) 4

Note how* takes precedence over MOD and DIV over + and –.

2 (a) FALSE   (b) TRUE   (c) TRUE
  (d) TRUE   (e) TRUE
3 (a) 8   (b) Frank's revision   (c) FRANK
  (d) evi   (e) 66
4 (a) Pear
  (b) Kiwi
  (c) fruit(1,1)
5 (a) 121, Fork 131, Spoon
  (b) 131, Spoon, 65, 1.15
  (c) 121, 56, 131, 65
6 SELECT "Item_No", "Description" FROM "tblstock" WHERE "Stock">'20' AND "Price"<'3.00'

Chapter 11

1 Any two from:
   – type
   – range
   – presence
   – format
   – length.
2 Whitelists contain inputs that are acceptable and all others are rejected.
3 Testing at the module stage as each module is developed and as modules are added to the program.
4 Any one from:
   – To check modules combine correctly.
   – To check that the final the program functions as expected.
   – To check the program produces the expected results with real data.
5 Error in the rules of the program.
   Any one from:
   – Variables not declared.
   – Variables not declared properly.
   – Incompatible variable types.
   – Assignments incorrect.
   – Variable names incorrect.
6 Run time error caused by the logical structure of the program. One from, e.g.
   – Division by zero
   – Programs that do not complete
   – The memory is filled with data and we get a stack overflow
   – Incorrect output
   – The program will crash*

Chapter 12

1 0

2 0

3

A	B	C	B AND C	P = A AND (B AND C)
0	0	0	0	0
0	0	1	0	0
0	1	0	0	0
0	1	1	1	0
1	0	0	0	0
1	0	1	0	0
1	1	0	0	0
1	1	1	1	1

4

A	B	C	NOT B AND C	P = A OR (NOT B AND C)
0	0	0	0	0
0	0	1	1	1
0	1	0	0	0
0	1	1	0	0
1	0	0	0	1
1	0	1	1	1
1	1	0	0	1
1	1	1	0	1

Chapter 13

1 The high-level code written by the programmer.

2 The machine code version of a program that the processor can run directly.

3 Computer processors work in binary; code is often written in a high-level or assembly language that cannot be run by the processor.

4 Any three from:
   – editor
   – debugging tools
   – step-by-step run through
   – a build feature to link other routines
   – a translator (compiler/interpreter)
   – run-time environment.

5 A simulation or emulation of a computer platform or system that enables programs for one platform to be run on a different one.

Chapter 14

1 (a) 13   (b) 161   (c) 204
2 (a) 00100011 (b) 10100111 (c) 11001000
3 (a) 01100000 (b) 11001011
4 (a) 11100000 (b) 00110011
5 (a) 3B   (b) C7   (c) FB
6 (a) 01001001 (b) 01011100 (c) 10101101
7 (a) 92   (b) 166   (c) 175
8 (a) 55   (b) A4   (c) AF
9 11110001. It has an odd number of 1s, the others have an even number of 1s.

Exam practice answers

Chapter 1

1 (a) Cache stores data waiting to be used by the CPU and frequently used data. The more cache memory, the more of this data that can be stored. Since access to cache is very fast compared to main memory the more cache memory the faster the computer.

 (b) Any two from:
  - Clock speed: the higher the clock speed the more instructions can be processed in a given time.
  - Cores: multiple cores allow for instructions to be processed simultaneously so the more cores there are the more instructions that can be processed every clock pulse.
  - RAM: with more RAM more data can be stored ready for use by the CPU avoiding slow data transfers.

2 The MDR stores data that is fetched from memory and data that is to be transferred to memory.

3 Small, fits into a small drone. Light, minimises the weight of the drone, robust, can withstand landing/crashes/movement in the air. Low power, only a small drain on the drone power supply, can fly for longer/reduces battery weight.

Chapter 2

Shirley's computer has only a small amount of RAM and she is using several applications. This means the computer is using virtual memory (a section of the hard disk) as if it were RAM. This means there are lots of slow data transfers between RAM and the hard disk. Adding more RAM will reduce these transfers and improve the performance. (Possibly also replace the magnetic hard disk with a solid-state device with higher capacity.)

Chapter 3

1 Secondary storage is needed to keep data and programs that would be lost if the power was turned off including the operating system, applications and user's data files.

2 Given the harsh environment, a medium not subject to damage from movement in extreme conditions, therefore SSD.

3

2 × 5-minute MPEG videos	=2 × 5 × 50	= 500 MB
3 × 3-minute MP3 music files	=3 × 6	= 18 MB
3 × postcard-size photographs	=3 × 6	= 18 MB
	Total	= 536 MB

This will fit onto a CD/RW, which is low cost and robust so can be posted to her friend.

Chapter 4

1 Any three from:
 - cables (UTP) to connect devices
 - switch to connect the computers
 - router to connect to the internet ISP
 - wireless access point to connect devices wirelessly
 - NIC to connect devices to the network.

2 Any two from:
 - Easy communication between users.
 - Files can be shared.
 - Peripheral devices can be shared.
 - Users can login to any connected computer.

3 One advantage from:
 - No messy wires.
 - No building work required.
 - Lower cost because no need for wires etc.

 One disadvantage from:
 - Signal can be intercepted so sensitive files vulnerable.
 - Slower speed than wired.

Chapter 5

1 Self-healing, with so many possible routes a single point of failure won't crash the network.

2 The channels overlap and can interfere with each other so we use three or four channels that do not overlap to avoid interference.

3 Each layer operates independently from the others.

 Each layer communicates with the one above and the one below.

4 Each layer is developed and maintained independently.

Modifying one layer does not require the others layers to be modified.

5 POP is used to retrieve email from a remote server. It generally moves the email from the server to the client computer.

IMAP allows complete management of the remote mailbox.

Chapter 6

1 Anti-malware software minimises the danger from malicious software being introduced onto the system. It looks for known malware and identifies suspicious patterns and features associated with malware. It removes any malware identified and prevents any new malware from being introduced.

2 Any two from:
 - Use of passwords and access levels for staff.
 - Firewall to control access to and from the network.
 - Physical security for devices.
 - WiFi security.

3 Any two from:
 - Web: don't download anything.
 - Email: don't open emails from unknown sources, or images or links or files.
 - Passwords: change frequently, use strong passwords, don't write them down.

Chapter 7

1 Over time the files on the hard disk get broken up into fragments scattered across the surface of the disk. This happens because files are deleted leaving gaps of varying sizes. This can result in larger files being stored in a number of locations in the available spaces on the drive. Because the read/write heads on the drive will have to move a lot to locate all the segments of the file, it will slow down access quite considerably. Defragmenting tools reorganise the files on the surface of the disk so that individual files and free spaces are put together.

2 Advantages: faster backup, requires less space, does not store duplicate files.

Disadvantages: slower restore, requires full backup + incremental backups to restore data.

3 Multi-tasking is the apparent ability of a computer to run more than one program at a time. The CPU switches between tasks so quickly the user is unaware of the process. As a program is waiting for data from a slower source, the process is moved to a waiting status and a program that is waiting is given processor time.

Chapter 8

1 – Security must be in place to prevent unauthorised access to the data.
 – Data may not be transferred outside the EU unless the country has adequate data protection legislation.
 – Data should be accurate and up to date.
 – Data should only be kept for as long as necessary.
 – Data should be relevant and not excessive.

2 Creative Commons is an organisation that issues licences allowing the user some rights, under described circumstances, to modify and distribute software.

3 One advantage from:
 – Targeted advertising may be useful.
 – Kept informed of events or topics of interest.
 – Large-scale collection of medical data can lead to new cures.
 – Collection of data may prevent criminal or terrorist acts.

One disadvantage from:
 – Advertising may become intrusive, e.g. spam emails.
 – Intrusion into private life.
 – May identify behaviour/ issues that the individual would prefer to remain private.

Chapter 9

1

0	1	2	3	4	5	6	7	8	9	10
A	B	D	E	F	K	L	M	N	P	X
L				M						U

Discard the lower section, midpoint is (6+10)/2 = 8

0	1	2	3	4	5	6	7	8	9	10
A	B	D	E	F	K	L	M	N	P	X
						L		M		U

Discard the upper section. New midpoint is (6+7)/2 rounded to 7

0	1	2	3	4	5	6	7	8	9	10
A	B	D	E	F	K	L	M	N	P	X
						L	M/U			

Item found at position 7

2 (a)

C	D	B	A

C	D	B	A

D and B out of order swap made.

C	B	D	A

D and A out of order swap and restart.

C	B	A	D

C and B out of order swap made.

| B | **C** | **A** | D |

A and C out of order swap made.

| B | A | **C** | **D** |

Restart.

| **B** | **A** | C | D |

B and A out of order swap made.

| A | **B** | **C** | D |

From here it completes the pass with no more swaps and, since a swap was made it restarts the process.

At the end of the next complete pass no swaps are made and it stops.

(b)

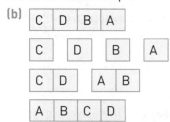

| C | D | B | A |

| C | D | B | A |

| C | D | A | B |

| A | B | C | D |

(c)

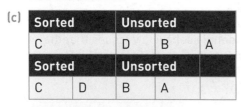

Sorted		Unsorted		
C		D	B	A

Sorted		Unsorted		
C	D	B	A	

Sorted	Unsorted		
B	C	D	A

Sorted			
A	B	C	D

3 Someone cannot be both less than 5 and greater than 16 so change >16 to <16

When this change is made it does not include someone who is 5 years old, it will charge them full fare

So we need to change >5 to >=5 to charge them half fare, OR if age >= 5 to let them ride free of charge.

```
input age
if age<5 then free
elif age >=5 AND age <16 then half price
else full fare
endif
```

Chapter 10

1 A label used to identify a location in memory holding data for a program.

2 The program can change the data stored in a variable, but it cannot change the data stored in a constant.

3 0,0   1,1   2,4

4
```
open "names.txt"
  for r = 0 to 2
    for c= 0 to 3
    write to file names(r,c)
    next c
  next r
  close "names.txt"
```
OR SIMILAR, it is the logic that is important.

5 (a) Birmingham, 1100

(b) Paris, France Barcelona, Spain

(d) SELECT "City", "Pop" FROM "tblCities" WHERE 'Currency"='EURO'

(e) SELECT * FROM "tblCities" WHERE "City" LIKE 'B%' AND "Pop" <'1000'

6 (a) 24

(b) "nct"

(c) "nd Pr"

(d) text.substring(5,4)

7 (a) A function always returns a value; a procedure need not return a value.

(b) Any three from:
 – They can reduce the overall size of the program.
 – The use of named subprograms can make the code easier to understand and maintain.
 – They only need be written and tested once saving time.
 – The use of subprograms improves debugging because code need only be checked in one place.
 – There are many pre-written and tested procedures and functions that can be reused minimising testing, saving time/ minimising the chance of errors.

Chapter 11

1 (a) division by zero when y=0

(b) logical

(c) Swap lines 4 and 5 so that divisor never reaches zero.

```
x = 100
y = 10
while y >0
    t = x/y
    y = y - 1
    print t
endwhile
```

2 Example only

Test	Data Used	Reason for test	Expected outcome
Valid	1.20	Valid price	1.44
Invalid	-2.00	Cannot have negative prices	Reject input
Extreme	0	0 lower limit of possible range	0
Erroneous	Apple	Non-numeric	Reject

3 Whitelist input sanitisation provides a list of acceptable inputs, all others are rejected. This is restrictive but very secure since no unacceptable input is possible.

Blacklist sanitisation uses a list of unacceptable inputs, all others are accepted. This is less restrictive but unacceptable inputs not on the black list are not rejected so less secure.

4 Any three from:
- Logs showing the tests that have been carried out and the results will enable the maintenance programmer to eliminate these as sources of error and simplify the process of tracking down bugs.
- In the code, indenting the program structures will enable a maintenance programmer to follow the process more effectively, identifying loop entry and exit points.
- Adding comments to the code will identify what each section does and how the program is intended to work.
- Meaningful variable names will help identify the purpose of each variable so that the maintenance programmer can see much more clearly what data should be expected at each point.

Chapter 12

1 1

2

A	B	P= A AND NOT B
0	0	0
0	1	0
1	0	1
1	1	0

3 (a)

A	B	P
0	0	1
0	1	0
1	0	0
1	1	0

(b)

A	B	C	P
0	0	0	1
0	0	1	1
0	1	0	1
0	1	1	0
1	0	0	1
1	0	1	1
1	1	0	1
1	1	1	1

Chapter 13

1 Any three pairs from:

Interpreter
- Translates a line at a time.
- Errors are reported line by line as they are processed.
- The source code is made available to the user.
- The user requires a copy of the translator in memory to run the program.
- The code runs more slowly than compiled code.
- The code does not get optimised.
- The code can be run on any machine with a suitable interpreter.

Compiler
- Translates the whole source code in one go.
- Errors are produced as a long list after compilation.
- Only an executable file is made available to the user.
- There is no need for a translator to be in memory to run the code.
- Compiled code runs faster.
- Compilers optimise the code to make it more efficient and effective.
- Compiled code is specific to a processor and will not work on another type.

2 One comparison from:

High-level languages are similar to human language and are translated into machine code by a translator. Assembly languages use mnemonics. Machine code is in binary.

Each high-level command is equivalent to several machine instructions. Each low-level command is equivalent to one machine code instruction.

High-level languages can be translated for various processors. Machine code commands can only run on the processor they were developed for.

3 The compiled code is virtually unreadable so it is difficult for a user to modify the code.

This provides some protection for intellectual property. The code can be run on the target environment without the end user needing a suitable translator.

4 Using an interpreter while developing code means the developer can run the code one line at a time to debug the code or try out ideas.

Chapter 14

1 (a) 11000001   (b) C1

2 (a) 00110100

(b) 00000011

(c) 110100 = 52, 11= 3

(d) 13/4 = 3.25, the shift has lost the last 1 in the number leading to underflow and an inaccurate result.

3 (a)

	1	0	0	0	1	1	1	0
+	1	1	0	0	0	0	0	0
(1)	0	1	0	0	1	1	1	0
1								

(b) 142+ 192 = 78

(c) The result has overflowed the 8-bit binary number.

4 All the characters available to a computer.

5 The higher the bit depth and sample rate the better the sound and the larger the file needed to store the sound.

6 The number of bits per pixel. It determines how many colours can be stored.

7 Any two from:
 - Lossy compression reduces the file size more than lossless.
 - Data can be downloaded more quickly.
 - More data can be stored on the same medium.
 - (The data loss is not noticeable.)